LET GOD LOVE YOU

Lloyd John Ogilvie

WORD BOOKS, Publisher, Waco, Texas

First Printing, January 1974
Second Printing, April 1974
Third Printing, August 1975
Fourth Printing, April 1976
Fifth Printing, August 1976

LET GOD LOVE YOU
by Lloyd John Ogilvie

ISBN 0-87680-353-2

Copyright © 1974 by Word, Incorporated
Waco, Texas 76703

Scripture quotations which are not identified by translator are from the
Today's English Version of the New Testament. Copyright © American
Bible Society 1966.
Scripture quotations marked RSV are from the Revised Standard Ver-
sion of the Bible, copyrighted 1946 (renewed 1973), 1956 and © 1971
by the Division of Christian Education of the National Council of the
Churches of Christ in the U.S.A. and are used by permission.
Scripture quotations marked Phillips are reprinted with permission of
Macmillan Publishing Co., Inc. from *The New Testament in Modern
English* by J. B. Phillips. © J. B. Phillips, 1958, 1960, 1972. Scripture
quotations marked Moffatt are from *The New Testament, A New Translation* by James Moffatt. Copyright © 1964 by James Moffatt. Used by
permission of Harper and Row, Inc. and Hodder and Stoughton, Ltd.

Library of Congress catalog card number: 73-91546
Printed in the United States of America

*To my gracious wife, Mary Jane,
with whom I have discovered that to
love God is to let God love you*

Contents

Preface

I want to write this preface as if we were able to sit down together and have a relaxed conversation. I want to tell you why I wrote this book and what I hope it will mean to you. When I have a chance to talk deeply with fellow adventurers in the Christian life, I often hear them ask how they can stay alive in a dynamic relationship with Christ and become effective and contagious communicators of love. Most often the conversation drifts into the need for a daily time of relevant, practical, personal Bible study and prayer. So many people have expressed the need to find a way to understand the Bible and come alive to its implications for the relationships and challenges of life at home, on the job, and in the tensions of society. This daily devotional guide is in response to this authentic, honest admission of need.

The theme which runs through all these pages dramatizes one of the deepest discoveries of my life. I have had a long, often disappointing journey in my search for the abundant life Jesus promised in the midst of religion and religious people. I can now clearly discern the difference between religion as man's effort to placate and please God and life as it was meant to be lived in Jesus' style. Increasingly, I am experiencing the delight of true faith as a response to God's love in Christ. I am discovering that to love God is to let God love me. The result has been an unbelievably winsome and joyous experience of daring to love myself as I am loved by God. This has overflowed in a new, gracious acceptance and enjoyment of people. As I allow God to love me, I have been amazed by the way he is able to take the raw material of my problems and potentials for fresh evidences of his providential, serendipitous grace. Therefore, a liberating formula for daily living has emerged as the basis of my life: To love God is to let God love you; to let God love you is to let him know you; to let God know you is to be open to him; to be completely open is to discover his exciting strategy for life. This flows naturally into a whole new quality of relationships: To love people is to let them love you; to let them love you is to let them know you; to let them know you is to be open about your hurts and hopes; to be open means to be vulnerable. This is what my study of Philippians has meant to me. I hope for nothing less for you.

The weeks of prolonged study in Paul's letter to the Philippians has been at once a rewarding and an alarming experience. A sustained effort to understand this epistle results in a deepening of the conviction of the reality and truth of the Christian faith as the source of answers to life's most existential questions. At the same time, the epistle exposes a devotion to Christ which makes our own seem flickering and fitful and reveals a joy which makes our fleeting lust for happiness seem puny and pitiful. The epistle stirred me to the depths and set me free anew to join with Paul and those to whom he wrote to "Forget what is behind me and do my best to reach what is ahead. So I run straight toward the goal in order to win the prize, which is God's call through Christ Jesus" (Phil. 3:13).

Here is a hymn to life. The music of the rhetoric is deeply appealing because the theme breaks through the dissonances of difficulties, loneliness and pain. There are no glib answers to mock our authentic search. What Paul writes, he has lived . . . and so must we! His letter reveals a conscious relationship to a living Lord. The service of Christ is in every sphere of his life; the Spirit of Christ is the temper of his mind; the perfection of Christ is the goal of his efforts; the power of Christ is the secret of his triumph. Here in the unstudied phrases of a love letter to trusted friends, we meet Paul personally and learn how to savor the wonder of the new life to which we have been called, and to sing a new song in the dark nights of life's discouragements and disappointments.

No one can read this letter seriously without repeating Richard of Chichester's prayer, "To know Christ more clearly, to love Him more dearly, and to follow Him more nearly."

As I wrestled with questions people often ask me and with Paul's answers, and tried to find ways of making the truths come alive, I came across some words of the psalmist which both described my experience and expressed my hope—

> I was dumb and silent,
>   I held my peace to no avail;
>   . . . .
> As I mused, the fire burned;
>   then I spoke with my tongue.
>   Psalm 39:2–3, RSV

"We shall meet again at Philippi" is a line from the grim dialogue between Brutus and the ghost in Shakespeare's *Julius Caesar*. They did meet again—it was in 42 B.C. when Brutus and Cassius were defeated by Octavian and Mark Antony in revenge for assassinating Julius Caesar. Disastrously defeated and in despair, Brutus fell on his own sword.

In a very different way, we too shall meet at Philippi. Our meeting, however, will not be with the Ghost of Death but with the Lord of Life. We will meet the colony of Christians who lived there years after the battle of Philippi, Paul who introduced them to Life, and the crucial letter he wrote to them.

It will be helpful to picture the strategic nature of the city of Philippi. There is a range of hills which divides Europe from Asia, the East from the West. That great chain of hills dips into a pass and affords an opening for the main road used in that day from Europe to Asia. The region was also important because of rich deposits of gold and silver. For these reasons, Philip of Macedon took the site from the Thasians about 360 B.C. He gave it its name, which means "Pertaining to Philip," and fortified it, making it the leading city in his realm.

In 16 B.C. Philippi fell to the Roman Conquest and became a colony as part of the Province of Macedonia. It was granted full rights of Roman citizenship and emerged as a center of Roman culture. As a "little Rome," it received Roman colonists who settled there along with parties of veteran legionnaires who were deployed at strategic road centers. They brought with them the pride and glory of Roman citizenship, government, customs, language, titles, and religion. They built pagan temples, perpetrated emperor worship, and continued to syncretize a multitude of diminutive Gods.

Because of its military and commercial position, Philippi was regarded as one of the most prominent cities of Macedonia. The Roman Road which ran through it brought to the city visitors of all races and religions. One of these was the Apostle Paul.

His concern for the Macedonians began in a dream during his second missionary journey, about A.D. 52. A Macedonian appeared in his dream and said, "Come over and help us." Saint Paul took the dream as a divine call and set sail from Troas across the Aegean Sea. He landed at Cavalla, then called Neapolis, and climbed the steep hill to the north of the port, descended part of the way to the plain on the other side, and walked on to Philippi. There he found the answer to why he had been called to Macedonia: Philippi was also strategic to the Lord and the expansion of the Faith.

I asked you to join me in an adventure of faith. Take fifteen minutes a day to become Christ-oriented and motivated. Use these minutes with the Lord to make the whole day alive with his power. Find a place where you can be quiet and then use this book as your guide.

Each day's devotional has been written to give you a Scripture for the day to read and think about. The opening thought for the day is a contemporary clarification of that Scripture. The meditations seek to dig out the deeper meaning of each passage and apply it to our lives today. I have tried to hear the questions we are all asking about God, our faith, our personal relationships, and how to make a difference in our world today. I pray that I have been neither trite with easy answers nor trifling with the love and trust an honest quest indicates. The prayer at the end is meant to be a starter. Use it as a launching pad to soar in your own conversation with our Lord.

Congregations may wish to use this devotional guide together. I used it in my church and preached a series of sermons on Philippians. The people were with me in a gratifying way as each day they considered an aspect of the Scripture I exposited on Sunday. I have tried to write this book in such a

10

way as to bring the study, fellowship, and worship of a congregation together around these biblical roots. It is anticipated that discussion and prayer groups could use this material as a study guide, utilizing the questions included in many of the days' devotionals.

I am profoundly indebted to my Administrative Assistant and treasured friend, Mrs. Norma Soll, for her help in preparing this manuscript, first for our congregation in Hollywood and now for this publication.

I agree with Zorba the Greek: "The only death is any day not devoted totally to living." But how? Paul answers, "For me to live is Christ!" So say I! It all begins when we let him love us!

The Viable Alternative

IT'S IN OUR RELATIONSHIPS THAT WE ARE
THE GOOD NEWS WE SEEK TO SHARE.

*From Paul and Timothy, servants of
Christ Jesus* (Phil. 1:1).

"It's not so much what you said . . . the new ideas or the different insights . . . that hooked me. It was the way you people
related to each other. I saw a quality of relationship . . . a style
of openness and freedom . . . a willingness to love the other
person with all his uniqueness and hang-ups. When I saw that,
listened to it, felt it, tested it, tried to blast it apart to no avail,
I knew what I was missing and why my faith was so ineffective.
You have given me a viable alternative!"

These words were spoken by a pastor at a National Clergy
Conference about a team of people who had been the leaders.
The man had been trying to preach, teach, and cajole people
into the Kingdom of God by good ideas. He had missed the
secret that the gospel is relational . . . it sets people in a new relationship to others. He had hoped to help people without deep
relationships; therefore the persons in his congregation were
unable to see the difference Christ could make in their relationships.

I am convinced that one of the reasons Paul was successful in
founding the church in Philippi was the relationship he had
with Timothy and the others in his missionary group. They
modeled the life they talked about. They were the gospel with
each other. As we read the account of their ministry in Philippi,
we see a remarkable style of life. In those few days they shared
a contagious love, healed a disturbed woman, sang and prayed
all night in jail in spite of beating and flogging, and witnessed
to Christ's power in such an attractive way that the children of
the new believers joined their parents in baptism.

13

Paul identified himself to the Philippians as a servant of Christ. The word was actually "doulos" in Greek, meaning slave. It expressed the basis of Paul's maturity in Christ as well as the essential ingredient of his relationships. A slave belonged body and soul to his master. His purpose and will was to obey. He was the absolute possession of his master. This enabled a great relationship with Timothy and his fellow workers and with the Philippians. Slaves relate on the level ground of a common bondage. How gracious of Paul to begin his letter to his friends in this way.

We all long to be part of a breed of people who love each other deeply, are committed to supporting each other, and are involved in a task together which constantly throws them into interdependence.

Who would want to know more of Christ because of the quality of our relationships?

> Lord Jesus, give me one person today with whom I can be absolutely open and real. Help me to be your incarnate love to that person and share what you mean to me and have done for me in my relationships. Help me to see that going it alone will eventually mean going it without you! Amen.

You Are A Saint

SAINTHOOD IS NOT STATUS, BUT ELECTION
TO SERVANTHOOD.

To all God's people living in Philippi who believe in Christ Jesus, together with the church leaders and helpers (Phil. 1:1).

"Now there's a real saint!" is an expression we use to pay a person a very significant compliment. By it we mean that a person

14

is living out his faith in spite of adversity or troublesome circumstances. We also refer to the apostles and great Christians of antiquity as saints. Often, we read of the Roman Catholic Church elevating a person of another period of history to sainthood, who had a vision of God and had performed certain spectacular, miraculous acts. But seldom do we think of ourselves as saints. And yet, this is one of the great New Testament designations of a Christian. It is the term Paul used in his greeting to the church at Philippi: "To all the saints in Christ Jesus who are at Philippi."

If we were addressed as Saint John or Jean or Sam, we would probably respond, "Oh yeah? You should know more about me and you wouldn't use the term so loosely."

Sainthood is not status. It has nothing to do with our achievement or impeccability. Rather, it reminds us that by grace alone God elected and set us apart to be his people. I think we should use the term more often because it clarifies for us that our goodness has absolutely nothing to do with earning what can only be received as a gift.

Consider the saints at Philippi. When we picture that church gathered together to listen to the reading of Paul's letter, we see an astonishing mixture of humanity. The church was a classless, inclusive, universal fellowship of very different kinds of people. And they were all saints—holy people—not that they were perfect, but that they were called and appointed to be God's people.

The three Philippians especially mentioned in Acts 16 are good examples. What a psychological and cultural cross section they represent! Lydia was an Asiatic, the slave girl was a Greek, and the jailer was a Roman citizen. Although very different, each had a similar experience of God's grace. Lydia seemed to be a spiritually sensitive sort, but it took the miracle of God's opening her heart to enable her to believe and experience his love. The slave girl's longing for reality was manifested in mediumistic powers. She saw in Paul the authentic power of God. At last, she was healed. The jailer was a down-to-earth, practical man whose life was simplified by a very mundane, unadventuresome job of tending a jail. He was probably not very spiritual by nature. Yet, when he witnessed Paul's faith in the test of crises, he wanted the power he saw in him.

God's love and presence are not given to a special few but to anyone who will open himself, surrender his will, and be obedient to whatever he is guided to do. Oh yes, there are some people who seem more naturally spiritual than others, but what does it say about God to suggest that he will make himself known only to them?

> Lord, I wonder at times at your call to me to be your person. I could not be a saint unless it means also to be a saint "in Christ." I belong to you, you live in me, and my courage comes from that. Show me any area where I am saying "no!" to you, or, "yes" to so many other loyalties that there is little time to abide in you. Make me more your person in thought, action, and reaction. I am yours, and by grace you are my Lord. Now what do you want me to do with this day? Amen.

What Is God Like?

GRACE IS WHAT GOD IS LIKE AND PEACE IS
WHAT HAPPENS WHEN YOU EXPERIENCE IT.

*May God our Father and the Lord Jesus
Christ give you grace and peace* (Phil.
1:2).

"Wow, God! Wow! It's too good to be true! But I know it's true for me now. Thank you for loving me just as I am and for replacing that uneasiness and fear I have always felt with a peace like I have never known before!"

This prayer was prayed by a brilliant young woman who had come to ask an academic question, "What is God like?" We talked in depth for several visits. How would you have answered from your own experience?

Paul gives us the answer in his greeting at the opening of his letter to the Philippians: grace and peace. What is God like? Grace! What happens to anxieties and fears when you experience grace? Peace! Paul's experience of God—his theology, message, and now his deepest yearning for his friends at Philippi —could be summed up in these two powerful words. But we often miss them because of our faithless familiarity with the words. Let's take today to rediscover the excitement the young woman expressed in her prayer.

Grace tells us what God is like in his attitude and action. The Greek word was used to express unreserved love for another out of pure generosity of heart and with no thought of reward. For Paul, grace was rooted in the cross. It can only be understood and experienced in the context of judgment. When we see what we have done with the gift of life, ourselves, people, the world; when the anxiety of separation from God because of our wilful rebellion finally gets hold of us; and when the knowledge that God loves us in spite of all that we have done or been amazes us—that's grace! It means forgiveness, acceptance, and a new beginning we never deserved.

Want to know what God is like? Look at the cross! As one man put it, "When I finally got past my blasted pride at being a good Presbyterian, worthy citizen, and magnanimous father and saw all the distorted motives and manipulative devices by which I lived, I could experience grace for the first time."

Peace is the result of grace. It literally means, "to bind together." In other words, the peace which comes from unmerited, unearned love can weave and bind our fragmented lives into wholeness. And the civil war of divergent drives, which makes us feel like rubber bands stretched in all directions, is ended. The Lord is in control. He has forgiven the past, he is in charge of now, and shows the way for each new day.

So, grace and peace to you!

Gracious God, thank you for showing me what you are like and what you want to do for me today. Help me to avoid the confusion of building up a religious jargon when you have told me all I need to know about you. I commit this day to live in your grace and peace. Amen.

Thanks For Being You!

THE CHRISTIAN LIFE IS BEING A GIFT.

I thank my God for you all every time I think of you; and every time I pray for you, I pray with joy, because of the way in which you have helped me in the work of the gospel, from the very first day until now (Phil. 1:3–5).

"She was a gift! That's the only way I can put it. She was a gift from God to me. She didn't bring gifts; she incarnated the one thing I needed: love and understanding!" That's the way a person expressed what she had found in a Christian friend who stood by her when others were too busy or turned away in judgment.

Our Christian life eventually becomes what we envision it to be. What if we were to think of ourselves as God's gift to others rather than as being obedient to a set of rules? How would we react to people if we thought of them as God's gift, some strangely wrapped to be sure, but each a unique gift to us as God's specific answer to our needs? When's the last time we thanked people for being a gift to us?

That thought stirs me at the core of my being. It breaks me open to deep levels of praise and thanksgiving which words cannot express. René Descartes said, "I shall be entitled to entertain the highest expectations, if I am fortunate enough to discover only one thing which is certain and indubitable." I have found that! God's love in Christ has been incarnated in a mag-

18

nificent procession of people who have marched through my life: my parents, the people who introduced me to Christ, my wife and children, the brothers with whom I have shared pastorates as teammates, the church officers who have maximized the triumphs and shared the trials of being the church, the adventuresome band of daring, contemporary saints across this country who share the vision of renewing the church and changing the world. My heart sings with unreserved praise to God! But do they all know how much they have meant to me? How can I tell them again in a way they can hear?

That was also Paul's concern. He wanted to leave no doubt about his gratitude. The opening lines of his letter express the profound appreciation he felt. It is almost inconceivable that he remembered them in his prayers. He had ministered to thousands in many places, yet he said he remembered them *all* in his prayers. One of the most expressive ways we can communicate how much we cherish another person is to pray for him and then let him know that we have.

I have found a helpful way of following through with people with whom I have talked about their needs. We establish a covenant to pray each day for that need and to keep in touch about what happens. Often the list gets long and the prayer time demanding, but it's a giant step for me toward being a person-centric church in a computerized society where even church members feel like numbers.

On the last Sunday of my ministry in Bethlehem, Pennsylvania, my son Scott put on his kilt, gathered his fellow bagpipers and piped me out of the church. It was a great moment of communication between father and son. I tried to express how I felt, "Thanks for the gift, Scott!" "What gift?" Scott asked. "The gift of being you!" was all I could choke out of my overflowing, Celtic heart.

> Lord Jesus, help me to refocus the meaning of the Christian life as being a gift and receiving others as gifts. You are the inexpressible gift of God's love, and in you we receive gifts of people beyond our deserving. Thank you. Amen.

So What's New?

GOD WILL FINISH WHAT HE HAS STARTED
IN US.

*And so I am sure of this: that God, who
began this good work in you, will carry
it on until it is finished in the Day of
Christ Jesus* (Phil. 1:6).

Can people change? Is it really possible for human nature to be changed? Is the promise we hold out to people that they can be different really true? What do we mean when we say that the old person fades and we become an entirely new person in Christ?

These are serious questions being asked today about the extent of personality change through faith, medicine, psychoanalysis, or any remedial effort of God or man.

Paul believed in the power of God to change human personality. The Philippians were living evidence of that. Yet they were people in process. Our verse for today expresses a powerful combination of affirmation and encouragement. He recognized the beginning and challenged the incomplete. How very sensitive!

Behind his confidence was his trust in Christ. He knew that the power of Christ was the life-changer. The words "began" and "complete" are sacrificial words. They designated the beginning and end of a sacrifice. The thought relates closely to Romans 12. "Present your bodies a living sacrifice, holy and acceptable to God, which is your reasonable service." Paul had offered his friends in Philippi as a sacrificial gift to Christ. He trusted their growth to him. He knew that their power to believe, any evidence of growth in their lives, and any sign of maturity in their personalities was because the Lord was at work in them. He now spurred them on to allow Christ to have his way with them.

20

People want to become the best we affirm them to be. Negative lambasting never changed anyone. Our improvement programs for people are not short-cuts to growth but sequacious paths on which they get lost. Paul believed that the shortest distance to personality change was a direct line to Christ. He knew that if he could assure the Philippians that Christ was at work in them, it would awaken grateful humility, out of which a new daring and aspiration would grow. It is in personal relationship with Christ that we change and become more like him.

I know this in my own life. It was because Christ had begun to work with me and gave me the gift of faith to respond that I started the Christian life as a college freshman. Radical changes in my personality and my relationships have taken place since then. I am not the man I was a few years ago; nor am I now what Christ will make me in a few months, tomorrow—today!

> Lord Jesus, you have exposed what human personality could be and gave me the promise that if I sacrifice all to you, I can receive the gift of becoming more like you in nature, thought, action, reaction, and attitude. I claim that today for my life. Continue what you have begun in me! Amen.

Sheer Delight

IN SPITE OF EVERYTHING, CHRIST DELIGHTS IN US!

You are always in my heart! And so it is only right for me to feel this way about you all (Phil. 1:7).

I have had an exciting experience with this verse. It has taught me how to take delight in being me. That's happened through the realization that, in spite of what I am at times and all that I have yet to discover, God takes delight in me. The result is a new delight about the people in my life.

One morning when I was studying this verse I was overcome with the realization of how delighted Paul was in the expression of his feelings for the Philippians. He knew all the problems and differences they were having, but his letter was written in the context of affirmation that they were "his people" regardless of what happened. It's one thing to talk about grace, something else to incarnate it. There is no evidence that he would hold back his feelings of joy over them until they measured up.

"You are always in my heart!" Paul wanted them to know the depth of his feelings. I am sure that the reason the Philippians were so open to Paul was because they felt the enjoyment he had in them. Real communication begins with delight in the person to whom we want to relate significantly.

One thing I have come to realize is that I often break the first commandment in my judgments. God created me in his own image. I return the compliment by the idolatry of making approval and acceptance a commodity to barter for the performance I want from people. After brooding over this passage for a long time, I took an honest inventory of the measure of delight people felt from me. I found that my feelings of delight were often measured out to match my standards.

The secret of Paul's delight in the Philippians was in his experience of God's delight in him. But there's also a subtle twist in the grammar of this verse which presents a fascinating picture of what the church should be. The expression, "Because I have you in my heart," could just as accurately be, "Because you have me in your heart." The Philippians were delighted in Paul, and this gave him courage throughout his ministry.

Who in your life and mine needs our delight? Life is short! Could it be that someone in our lives will never have that liberating experience? Why?

Lord Jesus, knowing all you do about me, I still get

the feeling you are delighted in me. How can this be?
I want this to be the motive for becoming the person
you long for me to realize. Help me to express delight
in someone in your name today. Amen.

How To Communicate

THERE IS NO EASY MAGIC IN COMMUNICA-
TION. IT IS BASED ON AN UNDENIABLE
SPIRITUAL LAW.

*For you have all shared with me in this
privilege that God has given me, both
now that I am in prison and also while I
was free to defend and firmly establish
the gospel* (Phil. 1:7).

Can you name twelve people with whom you can communicate
profoundly? People who really hear and understand you; people who can think and feel and empathize with you; people
who know what you're trying to say before you can put it into
words? I have asked that question of people of all levels of education and social status. There are few who can name even six.
Even great leaders and famed communicators whose business it
is to get through to people could mention only a person or two
with whom they felt they had ever been able to express their
true, inner self and be encouraged in an ambience of accepting
love. Would your experience contradict this?

Some time ago I determined to find out how to be that kind
of person. I studied all of the methods of winning confidence
and establishing trust. I experimented with all of the expressions,
attitudes, and facial contortions which were supposed to produce openness from people. Then one day I stumbled onto a

secret of communication which literally changed my life. In a time of personal need I shared a problem with an acquaintance with whom I had a very surface relationship. He listened intently as if we had suddenly entered onto holy ground. We had! When I finished, he thanked me because he said he had never been close to anyone in his life. Since that time, he has asked for help and talked things out with me many times. The secret is this: Don't wait for some magic gift, share what you are, dare to be vulnerable, and you will find people who count you among their deepest friends because you broke the communication barrier below the level of words.

Paul was free to share his life with people. The more you read his epistles, the more you feel his openness to be with people in weakness and strength, anger and affirmation. He was not "Mr. Perfect" in order to help people.

Some dear friends wrote their own marriage vows. What they said to each other expresses the basis of real communication: I take you as a gift from the hand of God, to be my wedded wife; and I promise in the presence of God and these friends to be your loving and faithful husband, in weakness and in strength, in sickness and in health, through hostility and affection, through tears and laughter, whether we be rich or poor, whether we succeed or fail, to the glory of God, as long as we both shall live.

> Lord, free me to be the kind of person with whom others can be real and personal. We are all part of a lonely crowd. Help me to be a communications initiator. Amen.

Love Is A Gift

WE CAN COMMUNICATE ONLY WHAT WE ARE IN THE PROCESS OF EXPERIENCING.

My deep feeling for you comes from the heart of Christ Jesus himself (Phil. 1:8).

As I sit in my study, I look out over the Lake Hollywood Reservoir surrounded by magnificent mountains. I am a few minutes away from downtown Hollywood and the Los Angeles area I serve. The water in the lake is portioned off each day for the needs of the city below. Often when I look out over the lake, I wonder how there can be enough water for the millions of people in the city. Early one morning I took a walk around the lake, and at the north end I was amazed to hear the rushing of water tumbling into the lake. I discovered that the rush of water came from the Colorado River and replenished the lake every day. What looks to me like a loch in a Scottish highland glen is really a widening in the passage of water from the Colorado River to faucets in the homes of Hollywood.

Loving is like that. I would like to be an endless resource of loving attitude and thought. I would like people to look at me as some do at Lake Hollywood and believe that I have an endless supply within myself.

Not so! The gushing, sparkling inflow of water is like the indefatigable inflow of Christ's love to me. I am a channel, not a reservoir.

This is why Paul was cautious to clarify, "My deep feeling for you comes from the heart of Christ himself. . . ." The Greek word used here is *splagchyna*, meaning "the bowels, upper intestines, heart, liver, and lungs." This was believed to be the seat of the emotions and affections.

Paul seemed to identify the source, spirit, and substance of his deep feeling of love for the Philippians as from Christ himself. Note that he did not say Jesus, but Christ Jesus. It was not the example of Jesus' loving life or death alone, but the power of the victorious, living Christ. There is a new fascination today with the historical person of Jesus as the "man for others." That's only the starting place. Jesus is the Christ; he is alive; he *is* the love we so desperately need for others.

25

Two things enabled Paul to say what he did to the Philippians. Paul knew that Christ loved them more than he ever could; his passion was to get that across in language they could understand and experience. Coupled with that was Paul's own personal realization of Christ's limitless love for him. We can only communicate what we are in the process of learning. The fresh discoveries of how Christ could deal with the raw material of his inadequate humanity overflowed in new love and affection for his friends. He did not chop love into separate categories, trying feverishly to decide whom he was loving and whom Christ was loving through him. When he had responded in thankful wonder to the love Christ gave him, then suddenly his hard, negative, judgmental nature was softened, and he fell in love with people. From that time on, his time, energy, money, learning, words, and emotions became the channels through which the Living Water flowed.

> Lord, lift me out of the frustration of trying to decide whether I am loving with your love, and help me to get out on a limb in caring about people. I know all along you will love through me in ways beyond my strength. Amen.

D.W.L.D.

SPECIFIC GUIDANCE COMES FROM CONTINUOUS RELATIONSHIP.

This is my prayer for you: I pray that your love will keep on growing more and more, together with true knowledge and perfect judgment, so that you will be able to choose what is best. Then you will be free from all impurity and blame on the Day of Christ (Phil. 1:9–10).

"I'll be praying for you," I said. "You will? Tell me what you are going to pray," responded the man who had related a complicated problem and was faced with discovering God's best among many confusing alternatives. Whatever he did, he would cause some person pain. The possibilities were not black and white, but gray . . . dull gray.

I looked at him intently before I answered his question. He wanted me to expose what I thought was best by how I was going to pray for him. Very honestly, I did not know and needed to level with him.

"I am going to pray that you have the gift of discernment." Then I told him about how Paul had taught me to pray for other people in today's verse. He did not give facile advice. He knew that the Philippians had profound problems as individuals and as a church. His prayer recalled them to the only source of guidance. I have learned that guidance is not a line on which we walk, but an ambience in which we live. Our relationship with the Lord is primary. Difficult decisions throw us back on him. What the Lord offers us is love, knowledge, and judgment in order to know what is best. Other translations of this verse use the words love, knowledge, and discernment.

Love guides us. If you loved the Lord with all your heart, what would you do? Which of the alternatives will enable us and all concerned to grow in the capacity to give and receive love? We have a formula in our family which reorients us. D.W.L.D. Do what love demands!

Next, knowledge enlightens us. This is the gift of revelation. It is God's particular application of his plan for us in a specific situation. We can ask, "Is what I want to do a part of God's revealed purpose for me in Christ? For the people I love? What would God decide in my situation? Will what I am going to do further his kingdom and his ceaseless activity of reconciling men to him and to each other?"

Then discernment—the capacity to make a judgment, a decision—clarifies the specifics. It is a gift experienced only in relationship with the Holy Spirit. An inner conviction of what is right begins to grow. In the breach of indecision we begin to have the assurance of what is right. We are able to do what we must regardless of the pressures of other people to fulfill their image of us. The Spirit gives us assurance even when our decision may seem absurd to others. We dare to move ahead un-afraid because even if we fail, our failures can never separate us from our Lord; and he can use them to help us grow and in-novatively turn them into a part of his strategy for us.

> Lord, you know the difficulty I have at times finding your guidance in life's decisions. Help me to open up to you completely and live in you so deeply that de-cisions will flow naturally out of that relationship. Help me to move out in faith, and know that you can use even my mistakes. Amen.

Bound To Be Free

THE BONDS OF CHRIST ARE FOR THE BINDS OF LIFE.

I urge you, then—I who am a prisoner because I serve the Lord: live a life that measures up to the standard God set when he called you (Eph. 4:1).

Perhaps it was the place that made the greeting so unusual. Two executives of a large corporation greeted each other in the luncheon room with a nonverbal gesture which started an amazing conversation with others who sat at their table.

As they approached each other, each lifted his left arm in the air, his fist closed as if tightly clasped by someone from above. The right arm was outstretched forward, the hand open wide. As we talked about this salute, we found that it was rooted in the idea of bondage to Christ and symbolized how Paul was bound by one hand to the guard with a short chain, called an

28

halusis, but his other hand was bonded to Christ. Paul was faithful in the bind of the chain because he was in the bonds of Christ. He was bound to be free!

These men are part of a group which meets regularly to sort out God's strategy in their lives. They face bonds of responsibilities, obligations, frustrations in their personal lives and complicated issues in society in which their relationship with Christ mandates concern and involvement. They work with fellow executives, friends, neighbors, disaffected youth, addicts, parolees, and religious agnostics who are in the church but out of faith. The bonds of Christ give them the courage they need. Like Paul, they are bond-servants of Christ and can say, "Hallelujah for the halusis!" Though he had spent most of the last years of his life in chains, en route to Rome or waiting for his trial there, Paul was one of the most free men who ever lived. He was able to face excruciating difficulty because he knew he belonged to Christ. Nothing or no one could change that.

This same remarkable freedom radiated in these twentieth century saints in business suits. With one hand bound to Christ they could say, "I belong to Christ, in spite of everything, in spite of my moods or feelings, in spite of my failures and distorted thinking at times." Then with the other hand they could willingly invest themselves in the painful bind of troubled people needing love and a city needing justice.

How about it? Can we reach up and accept the bonds of Christ and then reach out to touch lonely and alienated persons around us today? Christ will not let us go! And we cannot let go of those he has given us to love.

> Lord Jesus, whatever the constricting chains that life has dealt me, I pray to remain strong in the midst of them because I am in bondage only to you. Now in the quiet I hear you say, "I lived for you, I died for you, I was raised up for you, I am here for you—you belong to me!" Lord, I believe that and commit myself to communicate your love and live for your justice in my responsibilities today. Amen.

29

The Lord Of Circumstances

GOD CAN USE EVERYTHING THAT HAPPENS TO US.

I want you to know, my brothers, that the things that have happened to me have really helped the progress of the gospel (Phil. 1:12; read 2 Cor. 1:3–7).

"Lloyd, tell me, what's one of the most crucial discoveries you have made in the past ten years?"

I looked at the intense expression on my friend's face . . . he was not putting me on . . . he really wanted to know what had happened to me during the years we had not seen each other.

My answer came quickly, distilled by years of joy and pain, "Everything that happens to us is for what God wants to have happen to us; everything that happens to us is for what God wants to have happen to others, through us."

When pressed to explain, I realized how passionately I felt about my answer. If I have learned anything at all, it is to trust God with my circumstances. They are the raw materials of my greatest discoveries about God and what he is trying to say to me and to other people through me. I am constantly amazed at how God uses both the sorrows and successes of life in my communication of the gospel.

When Carlyle had finished the writing of one of his books, he said, "Never has there been a book which has come more direct and flaming from the heart of a living man." That's what the world longs to hear from us out of the fires of real life. Not pious platitudes, but life! Here's the secret: The reason for the rough places of life is to initiate us into the deeper wisdom of God and then through those experiences to become agents of his encouragement and comfort to others.

This is Paul's affirmation: The things he went through helped the progress of the gospel. He could have seen his imprisonment as curtailing his mission. Instead, he saw his circumstances as an *advancement.* The Greek words he used actually mean, "to cut before." The same term was used for the advance troops sent out ahead of an army to clear away the brush or any obstruction that was in the way of the free movement of the army. He felt that his experience was an advance clearing of the way and would make it easier for the Church to be bold and adventuresome.

Rather than saying, "Why did this happen to me?" Paul asked, "What is God saying in what's happening to me? How can he use this for the progress of the gospel?"

That's the essential question for today, isn't it? The progress—that is, the penetration and realization of the good news of God's grace in us and in the people around us—will come today by the way we live in rough or smooth places of life's circumstances.

> Lord, toughen my faith. I am soft and sentimental and want a magic escape from difficulties. I surrender all the sticky problems, the frustrating people, the impossible situations to you and ask you to help me to grow through them. Then, help me to be sensitive to share what you have given to me with the people who struggle and long for meaning all around me. Amen.

Contagious Christianity

WILLIAM JAMES SAID, "FAITH IS EITHER A DULL HABIT OR AN ACUTE FEVER."

The whole palace guard and all the others here know that I am in prison because I am a servant of Christ (Phil. 1:13).

"Wa'd ya want?" an exasperated waitress asked a couple of tired businessmen who sat down beside me at the lunch counter

31

in Washington National Airport. One of the men looked up and said, "Lady, I want a slice of life!" To this the waitress slammed down the menu and responded, "Buddy, that's the one thing I ain't got to give."

A slice of life! Life is the *one* thing we have to give. Life . . . not just a slice . . . but life in Christ. He told us he came to give us life. Our challenge is how to share this life with people. The admonition of the angel to the apostles after they were released from prison in Jerusalem encompasses the commission, the content, and the challenge of authentic evangelism. "Go . . . and tell the people all about this new life" (Acts 5:20, Phillips).

Whenever we press our ear to the New Testament—listen to the apostolic preaching, observe the church alive, feel the living Christ picking up his ministry where he left off at the ascension —there is Life! That's the dominant theme, the message that changed people and turned the world upside down. They told people *all* about this new life. But the life they shared was validated by the life they lived. New Testament evangelism was the communication of life.

It has been said that Paul's guards in Rome had to be relieved of that duty because they were all becoming Christians as a result of contact with him. This is validated by what he said about the creative use the Lord made of his imprisonment. Imagine being chained to Paul! The guards came to realize that Paul was chained to Someone else. Who was captive to whom? Paul was free in Christ and a prisoner for Christ's sake.

The privileges of a private residence and of having visitors were granted Paul. As the rotating guards watched over him, they were forced to listen to his conversation about life in Christ and they witnessed the quality of life he shared with others. Who could have resisted this exposure to the power of Christ?

The people who are a part of our lives are bonded to us for a reason. The question is: What do they find in us? What is the impact of our lives upon them? Why is it that often people know more about our political point of view, our personal prejudices, and our religious ideas than what it means to experience the adventure of life in Christ?

Lord Jesus, there are people who are bound to us in life's relationships—not chains, but loyalties, dependency, responsibility. We live in families and have people for whom we work and who work for us—people in trouble and people who trouble us. Who would know that we are alive in you? I willingly put myself in your bond, that with the other hand I may reach out today and communicate your life. Amen.

The Boldness Of The Bonds

BOLDNESS GROWS OUT OF CONFIDENCE.

And my being in prison has given most of the brothers more confidence in the Lord, so that they grow bolder all the time in preaching the word of God without fear (Phil. 1:14).

I talked to a man recently about how to live out his faith on the job. He had learned that a man in his office was not given a key promotion because of his outspoken beliefs. The man said, "The whole thing has made me afraid to speak out. But the most disturbing thing is that I now realize how important my position and salary are to me. I sense that my job is really a diminutive god for me. I find that, not only do I guard what I say now, but actually speak and act in ways that could diminish the possibility that anyone would know that I am committed to Christ."

My first reaction was to be critical or give advice, but as I listened intently, I realized that the man's problem is shared by all of us to some extent. There are times when all of us guard our flanks, move cautiously, and speak ambiguously.

As my conversation with my friend pressed more deeply, I realized that what he was doing was inseparably related to what

33

he was. He needed what the Christians at Rome needed when Paul came to stir their incognito, concealed, esoteric faith into new vitality. They had been a secret society—a shrouded band of frightened believers. Paul's witness gave them confidence and boldness. The two are related—boldness is always the result of new confidence.

We should keep quiet about our faith until we can't keep still! What I mean is—when the experience of our Lord's unchanging love is the confidence of our lives, we will be bold and not bland. People who have been healed by a miracle drug are not reluctant to tell you what saved their lives. Someone who is convinced of a political candidate doesn't have to be asked twice to tell you why. When we are wondrously in love, we want to talk about our lover. Possibly the reason we find it difficult to talk about what's happened to us in our faith is because so little has happened.

Most of the problems and frustrations of life we face are also troubling other people. If we share our faith as a theory, we touch no one where he is living. But when we talk about life and the confidence Christ has given us, there is communication. The burden to convince is replaced by the desire to care. As one man who was newly excited about Christ in his life put it, "I find that I now can be very open about what I am discovering. Often it's when I am in the midst of some new growth in my faith and dare to share what I am finding that I get through to people. My wife and I now want to live the kind of life in Christ that does not separate us from people. We want to be people whose daily life is so ordinary and natural, but so truly human, so alive with love and joy, so vulnerable to others, that every relationship is an opportunity to communicate the fantastic new thing that's happened since we turned our lives over to Christ's control."

Lord Jesus, my lack of boldness is related to my lack of confidence in you. Why is this? I know that nothing will happen through me until it happens to me, and that I can communicate only what I am in the process of learning. So Lord, set me on fire today

with a confidence which will inadvertently break the
sound barrier. Amen.

A Bad Case Of Eritheia

CHRISTIAN FELLOWSHIP IS MADE UP OF
PEOPLE WHO SEEK TO BE TO EACH OTHER
WHAT CHRIST HAS BEEN TO THEM.

*Of course some of them preach Christ
because they are jealous and quarrelsome,
but others preach him with all good will.
These do so from love, for they know
that God has given me the work of defending the gospel. The others do not
proclaim Christ sincerely, but from a
spirit of selfish ambition; they think that
they will make more trouble for me
while I am in prison* (Phil. 1:15–17).

A fellow clergyman tried to draw me into a vindictive conversation about a neighboring church. "They're not preaching the
gospel!" he said.

I tried to get him to explain what was missing in their proclamation and program. His answer was that the Scriptures were
being watered down and the true faith was not being offered.
Then he exposed his real feelings.

"Not only that. People are flocking to that church. We are
losing members every week to them."

When I asked if he had been to see his brother pastor as a
friend, he said that he had not and would not.

The man suffered from a serious spiritual sickness called
eritheia, a self-seeking, ambitious, competitive spirit. There is
some of that in all of us. Some of our most beneficent activities
are self-centered, and often our concern for others is a projec-

tion of self-concern. The real danger comes when we cannot recognize it or admit it. Once we do, we can confess it, seek Christ's healing, and be helpful to others who are still caught in its grip.

Not everyone was happy to see Paul come to Rome. There were some people called Judaizers who insisted that a person come to Christ through Judaism, and they were undercut by Paul's proclamation of justification by faith alone. His popularity caused them to be envious and critical. Their great concern was not Christ but their self-perpetuating cause. Paul uses a descriptive word to explain the pain this caused him. It brought a *thilipsis*, which means friction, an excruciating rubbing of the iron chains. His deepest concern for these troublemakers was that they were insincere.

The cause of conflict between Christians is an emphasis on the particulars and not the Person of the faith. Envy is the cause of criticism and judgment of one another. Think for a moment about the fellow Christians of whom we are critical. What's the real reason for our feeling? And what have we done to love these people back to the Lord of life?

How can we be a source of healing to people who suffer from eritheia? Perhaps a start would be to ask for the power to love them and share with them how we feel and what Christ has done with the same problem in us. Jealous ambition is a telltale symptom of an insecure state of grace. We need to minister to the cause rather than be discouraged by the symptom. Think of what could have happened to the people mentioned in our Scripture for today if they could have admitted to God and to Paul how they felt. They did not have to stay sick. Nor do we.

There is a wonderful story about a friend of Leonardo da Vinci who came to see the unfinished picture of the Last Supper. His attention was attracted to the beauty of two silver chalices on the table in front of Jesus. He exclaimed with excitement about the artistic skill portrayed in the chalices, completely ignoring the features and expression of the central figure of the painting. Leonardo's response was to take his brush and paint out the distracting chalices. "It is not that that I want you to see," he cried. "It is that face!"

36

And that's whom we want people to see in us today—not the secondary loyalties or convictions about causes or aspects of the faith which often we share more readily than Christ and his love.

> Thank you, Lord, for allowing us to see how much we need you. When we honestly admit the vestiges of our old ways of relating to life, we thank you that you love us as we are, but never leave us there. Amen.

The Authentic Test

CHRIST CAN USE EVEN OUR MIXED MOTIVES!

It does not matter! I am happy about it —just so Christ is preached in every way possible, whether from wrong or right motives (Phil. 1:18).

I have come to believe that one of the authentic tests of a man in Christ is his inclusiveness. The deeper he grows in Christ, the broader is his reach to enfold others who may express their faith and action differently. There is a tender lack of judgmentalism in a person who has suffered and experienced the forgiveness and new beginning of life in Christ.

We read today's verse with awe. How could Paul be so tolerant of people who preached Christ out of jealousy and ambition? I think it was because of a powerful mixture of passion for Christ, trust in his power to innovate good out of human failure, and acceptance of his own humanity. He wanted Christ to be made known in every way possible. He knew that he could not reach everyone. Others, for whatever motives, could get through to some he could never reach. He also trusted Christ to bring good out of the mixed natures of people. The patience of our Lord is magnificent in the way he waits for each of us to respond in different ways. Think of the strange ways that men

37

are brought to Christ. What is abhorrent to us may be just the answer for someone else.

But also, Paul could admit his own mixed motives. The pages of the New Testament are full of the evidences of his humanity: his curt dismissal of Mark, his conflict with Peter, his discord with the church in Jerusalem, his healing of the slave girl in Philippi because of her persistent harassment, his confession in Romans 7 that often he knew the good but could not do it. Yet Christ had done great wonders through him. He knew that he was in transition and had only begun to grow in grace.

Often people who have known life's pain and disappointment are able to express initiative love to others who fail. The flip side is that usually the things we see in others which we don't like are exactly what trouble us. When we listen intently to our criticism and judgments, we can tabulate what's wrong inside ourselves.

As we go through this day, let's make a conscious effort to evaluate the people whom we cut off because of their manner, style, ideas, or the expressions they use.

Lord, we confess our mixed motives. Even our relationship with you is motivated by self-concern. Our best effort at loving others is our own need to be loved. We surrender this to you and ask that you will motivate us from within by your indwelling Spirit of love so that we will be free of our need of things and people as the security of our lives. You alone can meet that need. Now show us how to use all that you have given us to love the people you have entrusted to us to enable and care for in your name. Amen.

How To Pray For People

THERE ARE RESOURCES OF GOD'S POWER TO BE RELEASED WHEN WE PRAY FOR EACH OTHER.

And I will continue to be happy, for I know that, because of your prayers and the help which comes from the Spirit of Jesus Christ, I shall be set free (Phil. 1: 18, 19).

A friend of mine was deeply troubled and exhausted, yet he had responsibilities he could not ignore. Some very rough days were ahead of him. "Listen," I said, "every time you tighten up and get anxious, remember I am going to pray for you once every hour these next few days. Remember, I've taken the burden for you and will consistently talk to our Lord about it. Go ahead and relax!"

When I heard from him some weeks later, he told me about an incredible freedom he had found during those days of pressure. When things got tight, he remembered I was praying and it gave him courage.

When we have similar experiences, we know that prayer for other people works. In our church in Hollywood we are discovering the power of intercessory prayer. Often on Sunday evenings in the sanctuary we gather for prayers for the healing of the physical, emotional, and interpersonal needs of people. The response has exceeded anyone's expectation, and God has answered prayers beyond our dreams. We have simply claimed James 5:13-18 about the power of prayer and the authority of the elders of the church to pray for God's healing power. The result is a new dependence on the power of the Holy Spirit. The healed bodies, relationships, memories, marriages, and problems of our people convince us that God is at work among us and the key to unlock his power for each other is prayer.

Paul asked the Philippians to pray for him. He said that their prayers and the help of the Spirit of Jesus would deliver him in his need. The unstudied rush of Paul's thought in this sentence gives us an insight into his deepest feelings about the power of prayer. He has two sources of strength: the Philippian prayers and the help of the Spirit of Jesus. Could it be that when he thought of their prayers he also thought immediately of the thing for which he most needed them to pray? The help of the Spirit—that's the supreme prayer we can pray for another.

We cannot explain it, but there are resources of God's power which are released only when we pray. Prayer is the language of partnership with God in his continuing work of reconciliation. We pray, not to change but to discover the will of God. Prayer draws us into fellowship with God and the people for whom we pray. He motivates in us the desire to pray for the very things he is more ready to give than we are to receive. The purpose of prayer is to unify us with God and each other.

Holy Spirit of God, I want to pray without ceasing and without reservation today. Thank you for the resources of power you give me for the people in my life today. When people march before my mind's eye just now, I want to pray for them one by one. The greatest need in each of them is for you. Help me to see beneath the strange wrapping of the problems to the inner need for your healing. I move into this day with a new confidence in the power of prayer to release the dynamic energies of your Spirit in people's lives. Amen.

How To Pray For Yourself

HOW WOULD YOU PRAY IF YOU KNEW CHRIST WANTED THE ANSWER TO YOUR PRAYER MORE THAN YOU DO?

For my deep desire and hope is that I shall never fail my duty, but that at all times, and especially right now, I shall be full of courage, so that with my whole self I shall bring honor to Christ, whether I live or die (Phil. 1:20).

40

A question which I have asked and enjoyed answering in discussion groups at conferences is, "If you had five uninterrupted minutes with our Lord, what would you say to him and what do you think he would say to you?" The value of the question is that it focuses our deepest desires and reminds us that those five minutes are available anytime. Another way to clarify that is to ask, "If you could have only one prayer answered, what would you pray for?" A flow of possibilities floods our minds. How would we choose?

One of the most liberating discoveries I have made in my own relationship with Christ is that he is *for* me and not against me. He wants the best for me! That's often difficult to accept because I am very demanding of myself. Whatever I desire to improve my life, Christ wants for me more than I could ever imagine.

In today's verse, Paul gives us both the mood and content of great prayer for ourselves. His prayer centered on his "deepest desire," or "eager expectation." The words in Greek literally mean, "stretching out the head." They picture a person with head erect and stretched forward, whose attention is turned away from all other objects and riveted upon one. This term was used in classical Greek to designate the watchman in the bow of the ship or in the crow's nest, who peered into the darkness, eagerly looking for the first sign of an orienting beacon—intense, concentrated hope which ignores all other interests. This is the attitude of personal prayer which urgently looks for Christ's guidance. The purpose of prayer is relationship, not answers. Anything we might receive as a result of praying is meager in comparison to our Lord's greatest gift . . . himself.

In this attitude, Paul asks for three things: that he never fail in his duty, that he be full of courage, and that he will bring honor to Christ. The fascinating thing about this prayer is that our Lord wanted that for Paul even more than Paul wanted it for himself. Christ was on Paul's side, but these qualities were gifts to be received, not prizes to be achieved. Paul did not want to be ashamed by failing in those last crucial days. He longed for boldness in speaking out for his Lord. His longing was to glorify Christ, to manifest his power, to be conspicuous in his witness. All of this he longed for whether he lived or died.

As I think about Paul's eager expectation, I know what I want for my life today. I long for the same things. I want to be faithful, bold, and to reflect Christ's love and power in all my duties. What about you? There's just enough time today to do the things he wants us to do in the way he wants us to do them.

> Lord, I eagerly stretch my attention for your reorienting beacon for today. What I need, you have offered to give me. I want to be your person today. Come live your life in me and enable me to live dependently, abandoned, to your unfolding strategy for my life. I want to speak for you or be silent for you, be active or rest at peace, live or die for your glory. Amen.

The "Now" Breed

TO BE A CHRISTIAN IS TO BE IMMERSED IN THE "NOW."

. . . and especially right now . . . (Phil. 1:20). *When anyone is joined to Christ he is a new being: the old is gone, the new has come. All this is done by God, who through Christ changed us from enemies into his friends, and gave us the task of making others his friends also* (2 Cor. 5:17, 18).

The woman could not, would not, forget. She recalled the details surrounding the incident of thirty-two years before with vivid detail. We talked in depth about the abortion. She could

42

not accept or forgive herself for what she called a "genocide," although she had been in church through these years, heard the assurance of pardon, and listened to the gospel of new beginnings. Her whole life in the present was clouded by memories of the past.

Do you ever find that the memories of past failures and hurts lurk in you? We are told that the mind is like a computer which stores up all that we have done or said and all that has been done or said to us. The resentments of the past, the broken relationships of the years, and the troublesome reminders of our failures all around us can rob us of the joy of living right now.

But what about worry over the future? Often our concern about what will be blocks out zestful enjoyment of what is now. Pascal said, "We are never living, but only hoping to live; and, looking forward always to being happy, it is inevitable that we never are so." We live our lives on a deferred payment plan. I agree with William James, "We do not live, nor enjoy life now, but wait for some future event or occurrence."

The bonds of Christ enabled Paul to live fully immersed in the now. In these words, "Especially right now," we hear Paul desiring to be the Lord's man in the present moment, completely alive to what the Lord was seeking to accomplish in that hour. He was free to actualize, to see the situation as it was; he was free to relationalize, to enter into relationships of gracious caring; and he was free to realize, to be sensitive and aware of what the Lord was seeking to do through him.

For Paul, newness was nowness. He was part of Christ's "now" breed. He believed that the old had passed away through the forgiveness of the past. The new had come! The manifestation of his being a new creation in Christ was that he could live fully in the moment at hand.

St. Catherine of Genoa discovered the secret. She took cognizance of things only as they were presented to her in succession, moment by moment. To her now-oriented soul, the divine moment was the present moment. When the duty was involved and accomplished, it was permitted to pass away as if it had never been, and she gave herself to see faces and duties of the moment which came after.

The Lord is more concerned with the process than the product. He is never finished with us; we are forever becoming. The process will go on in eternity. In Christ we are alive forever. Our forgiveness was settled on the cross; our future was secured by the resurrection. That frees us to live today with celebration and joy.

> Lord of the now, I want to express my excitement over the gift you have given me to live completely in each moment. Thank you for settling the past with forgiveness and the future with assurance. I am delighted to be alive and want to use each hour of today to sense and feel, listen and love, enjoy and savor the gift of life. Amen.

Become What You Are!

CHRISTIANITY IS LIFE AS CHRIST LIVED IT,
LIFE AS WE LIVE IT IN HIM, AND LIFE AS
HE LIVES IT IN US.

For what is life? To me, it is Christ!
(Phil. 1:21).

Recently, I taught a seminar at a conference on the theme, "How to Become a Christian." I was amazed at how many church members attended. One man expressed the feelings of many: "I have always wanted to find out how to become a Christian but was afraid to ask." I have talked with people associated with the church all over the country who have longed to ask the question about how to discover the reality of the faith.

Paul's exclamation of the core of his faith gives us a framework for an answer. "For me to live is Christ." Christ was Paul's life. Belief was more than the acceptance of truth or affirmation of the deeds of an historical figure. For Paul, Christianity was fellowship with a Person. Christ was his purpose, passion, and power. He was the foundation of his existence and the Lord of his life. How can we know Christ with that same assurance? How can we find him as our life?

1. Begin with the liberating fact that we would not be asking the question if Christ had not already found us. Jesus' words in Pascal's prayer are helpful to us: "Thou would'st not be seeking me had'st thou not already found me."

2. Consider what Christ has done for you. That's the gospel of his grace. Look long and hard at the cross and the initiative love he has for you. He suffered and died for you as if you had been the only person alive.

3. Confess your sin, that means more than sins, but the *separation* of your life from Christ. Tell him as honestly as you can what you have done to life and what it has done to you. Make a penetrating moral inventory and confess that you need to be changed.

4. Surrender control of your life and its future. Make a conscious commitment of your will, to seek and do his will.

5. Invite Christ to come and live in you. Give him your mind to think your thoughts, your body to be his home, and your emotions to express his love.

6. Thank him that he has answered your prayer, forgiven you, and now lives in you. Trust him and not your feelings.

7. Tell someone you have turned your life over to Christ. Make any restitutions which need to be cleared away to completely belong to him.

8. Ask Christ to reveal to you how to help others find what you have found and join him in some crucial activity of caring about people and their circumstances in society. Then you will be able to say with Paul, "For me to live is Christ."

> Lord, I want to go through these steps carefully for myself. Show me where I am in this personal inventory. Then help me to radiate the results of life in you so that I may be available to others who long to ask the same question if they knew they could find someone to answer. Amen.

A Deathless Life—Or Living Death?

WE MUST DIE TO LIVE.

Death, then, will bring something even
better (Phil. 1:21).

"You have no right to force me to think about death. I came to the Easter service to hear about the resurrection, not to be challenged about my own dying. I want to know how to live, not how to die!"

The man was disturbed. His directness made way for honest conversation about why talk of death was so unsettling to him. In the Easter sermon I had asked each person to picture his life—responsibilities and relationships. Then I asked, "What if you were told that you were to die today. How would you feel about it? Actually let yourself feel it! Do you have the assurance that death would only be a transition in living for you? Do you know the reality of the resurrection for yourself—not just for Jesus so long ago, but through him for yourself?"

The man was shocked by the realization that though he believed in Christ, he was afraid of dying. He could not say with Paul, "To die is gain." Fear about death and dying is evidenced by our customs for the funeral and our efforts to evade the eventuality of our own dying.

A congregation in the Midwest asked its members to provide data for the pastor's personal files on how each would want to celebrate his life in a Christian memorial service. They were thrown into turmoil because most people had never thought or felt through their beliefs about dying. For all the preaching, praying, hymn singing, and study about eternal life this company of believers had not experienced Christ as the vanquisher of death.

We cannot live—really—until we come to grips with death. Paul's statement to the Philippians about death was based on the previous phrase about life. He had died to himself and his own

46

wilful design for his life long before he made this statement in prison. Death was not an ending for him but the beginning of the next phase of eternal life which had begun when he turned his life over to Christ. "I have been crucified with Christ. It is no longer I who live but Christ who lives in me."

Once we have faced the fact of death, accepted Christ's promise, "Because I live, you shall live also," we are ready to turn back to the challenge of living with new zest and abandonment. Just as Paul turned to his responsibilities with new freedom once he had considered his death, so we will be free to live when we have passed from death to life. Goethe was right, "Those who hope for no other life, are dead even in this."

My Easter Christian picked up the challenge. We talked at length about his life. Now he doesn't have to wait until Christmas to come to church again. He's there every Sunday!

> Lord, free me from the fear of death. Take me back through the hidden recesses of my thoughts and show me why, with all I believe, I am often still afraid. Today I want to experience the reality of dying to my own control of my life and discover a quality of eternal life which death cannot end. Amen.

Discipleship By Objectives

WE ARE IN THE PROCESS OF BECOMING THE GOALS WE SET.

But if by living on I can do more worthwhile work, then I am not sure which I should choose. I am caught from both sides: I want very much to leave this life and be with Christ, which is a far better thing; but it is much more important, for your sake, that I remain alive. I am

sure of this, and so I know that I will
stay. I will stay on with you all, to add
to your progress and joy in the faith
(Phil. 1:22–25).

If you had to explain to one other person what are your ultimate, long-range and immediate goals, could you do it?

We hear a lot about goal-oriented planning, management and task accomplishment these days. Peter Drucker coined the phrase, "Management by objectives," and reminded us that we become the goals we set. The three levels of goals—ultimate, long-range and immediate—are interdependent and enable each other. Our ultimate goal clarifies the long-range goals, but the immediate goals, what we do today or this week, determine our progress toward our purposes.

In our Scripture verses for today, Paul lets us into his intimate reflection about his goals. His parenthesis, or what some would call his throw-away lines, give us the feeling of the man. In the carefully worded flow of thought in his letter, he pauses to talk to himself, in a way, about what is best for his life to fulfill his goals. We are ushered into the inner chambers of his spirit to consider with him a very strategic inventory of his life's purposes.

Paul clarified again his ultimate goal—to live in Christ. Nothing could ever dissuade or destroy this reason for his being. In that context he could evaluate the long-range goals in his ministry. Should he remain alive, it would be to take the next step of strengthening the churches he had begun and take the next strides in expanding the kingdom to unreached areas. He had a reason for living on, even though death would be a pleasant beginning of a new phase of his life in Christ. We feel a man sorting out the priorities of his immediate decisions on the basis of how they would bring him closer to his long-range and ultimate goals.

The cause of confusion in the lives of many Christians today is because immediate tasks are put in the category and given the importance of ultimate or long-range goals. We are pulled from demand to demand with little basis for sorting out what's most important. Also there are many who get long-range and ulti-mate goals mixed up.

Take my ministry for example. To communicate the viable adventure of the new life in Christ, help people to meet him and discover a ministry of their own, and challenge them by giving innovative leadership to the fellowship of the church is my long-range goal. It's not my ultimate goal. If I have a ministry only because I am in "the ministry," then I do not have an authentic ministry.

I should be able to change my vocation without altering my ministry. My ultimate goal is to be a man "in Christ"—to love and sense him with all that I am and have. The long-range goal is to do that by the ministry of communicating Christ to others. On the other hand, my immediate goals deal with the people and program which demand attention right now. No cause, however strategic, should ever be elevated beyond a short-range classifica-tion. Like Paul, we can decide on the value of any one chal-lenge by how it will bring us more closely to our real purpose.

> Lord Jesus, thank you for giving my life the ebullient joy of an exciting ultimate goal of glorifying you and enjoying you forever. In the light of that, help me to check the long-range goals to which my life is mov-ing. Help me to sort things out for today in order to make the day count as a significant step toward my life's goal. Amen.

Braggin' On The Lord

PRAISE IS A HEALTHY EXPRESSION OF AU-THENTIC PRIDE.

So that when I am with you once more you will have even more reason to be

proud of me, in your life in Christ Jesus
. . . (Phil. 1:26).

I have had a difficult time learning how to be proud in the right
sense. There is a real difference between creative pride and false
pride; one is the result of grace, the other a lack of it. The quality of the pride we feel is an expression of the nature of our
relationship with our Lord. Pride is either defensive or demon-
strative; it is either a wall of protection against the invasion of
our insecurity or a projection of our security.

I can remember the normal pain of growing up. At one stage
of my late teen years, I was arrogantly proud of a few accomplishments in the world of speech and dramatics. I clutched my
trophies, awarded as the result of national oratorical and decla-
mation contests. These were tangible signs to me of my worth
as a person. My lack of inner self-appreciation was expressed in
insufferable pride which almost became a personality pattern. At the same time, childhood training and conditioning in a
mixture of biblical teaching and Celtic discipline declared civil
war within me on any kind of self-satisfaction.

After I became a Christian, I was amazed to find that the
Scriptures talked about another kind of pride. It was the pride
of fulfillment. I noted how often in his letters Paul talked about
people being his pride and joy in the Lord, and I remember
especially how mixed my feelings were when I first read our
verse for today. I felt Paul had lapsed back into momentary self-
justification or had defected from graciousness when he ac-
knowledged that the Philippians would have reason to be proud
of him. The word leaped off the page. The only thing I could
imagine which was worse than self-pride was to want others to
take pride in you. I tenaciously resisted any temptation to be
excited about the good things that happened to me because I was
afraid to take credit for them myself. The result was pride in
not being proud. I had justified myself before God . . . or so I
thought.

But God has been tenderly kind through the years. Early in
my growth in Christ a friend taught me how to do what he
called "braggin' on the Lord."

It was a genuine relief to express an enjoyment of life and pleasure at achievement, knowing that it was all possible because of what the Lord was doing in my life. I felt particularly free when I no longer had to distinguish between what I had done on my own power and what the Lord had done for me. He had made it all possible.

Note that Paul says that the Philippians will have reason to be proud of him in "Christ Jesus." He uses this name when he wants to stress not just the historical manifestation of the power of God, but the present sphere in which the same blessings are enjoyed by the Church as were incarnated in Jesus of Nazareth.

Therefore, to be proud "in Christ Jesus" is to acknowledge that he is the benefactor of the blessings we enjoy. He is the Giver of our gifts, the Author of our profound thoughts and expressions, the Source of the serendipities of life. Thanksgiving grows out of a realization that all our capacities are entrusted to us and all that has happened has been arranged by Christ's infinite goodness.

One evening my daughter, Heather, came into the living room before going out to a special formal dance. She spun around in joyous self-affirmation and exclaimed, "Daddy, I'm glad I'm me!" Can you say that?

We can be proud of ourselves, other people, and our accomplishments because we know that nothing would be possible without God's provision. Therefore, we can be proud of the things we say or accomplish, the children we have, or the positions we hold. Creative pride, then, is praise!

This a day for pride . . . let's keep a record today of the people, situations, and developments which are the motivation of authentic pride.

Lord Jesus, it is a burst of new freedom for me to be unashamedly proud of all that has happened to me. You are the source of it all. I praise you for what you have been willing and able to do with me. Thank you for liberation from defensive arrogance and for the joy of praise to you for all that I have and am. Amen.

51

BE CAREFUL TODAY TO BE SURE THAT THE
BATTLE YOU ARE FIGHTING IS THE LORD'S
BATTLE!

*Now, the important thing is that your
manner of life be as the gospel of Christ
requires, so that, whether or not I am
able to go to see you, I will hear that you
stand firm with one common purpose,
and fight together, with only one wish,
for the faith of the gospel. Never be
afraid of your enemies. This will prove
to them that they will lose, and that you
will win—for it is God who gives you
the victory! For you have been given the
privilege of serving Christ, not only by
believing in him, but also by suffering
for him. Now you can take part with me
in the fight. It is the same one you saw
me fighting in the past and the same one
I am still fighting, as you hear* (Phil.
1:27–30).

"Don't forget . . . the battle is the Lord's!"

This is the way a friend of mine ends all of our conversations. I am never sure whether he thinks I need to realize this, or that he needs to remind himself. Probably both! We all need to take an inventory of life's battles to consider which are ego skirmishes for our control of situations or people and which are the Lord's battles for justice and truth.

A woman said to me, "You know, I have lived the past fifteen years of my Christian life thinking that God belonged to my political party, had the same plans for our community that I had, and was against all the things I was against. Now I am not so sure. . . ."

The Psalmist made the same shocking discovery, "Oh thou Eternal . . . who would not march out with our army" (Ps.

60:10, Moffatt). There are times when our best-laid plans do not seem to have God's sanction, and he will not march with the armies of our convictions to the cadences of our preconceptions and prejudices.

My friend was right. We need to be sure that we are fighting the Lord's battle. In the renewal of the church, we all get exercised about changes which are little more than a rearrangement of the status quo. The Lord is up to greater things than the order of the worship service or the color of the sanctuary carpet or even the wording of our theological statements.

Paul was concerned that the Philippians get into the right battle. His hope was that they would fight together with one common purpose, one wish, for the faith of the gospel. He wanted them to fight the Lord's battle in the world, rather than fight with each other within the church. The words, "For the faith of the gospel," give us a good plumb line on the conflicts of our life. How many of them have been motivated, guided and empowered by the gospel? Can we fight one battle with one wish and one purpose with others who also love the Lord?

The war against the church in Philippi had been declared years before when Paul preached the gospel there and nurtured the new church to life. It had never been popular to be a Christian in Philippi. The cosmic battle of the Lord with the power of evil had been engaged there as well as anywhere the gospel had been preached. The church's battle was for the minds and souls of the people in spite of punishment and persecution. In fact, if we are not in some battle for the Lord, we are probably not very conspicuous for what we believe.

It's great to fight a battle knowing that we will win. Paul says, "Never be afraid of your enemies." The reason for this fearlessness is that he believes God won the victory over the three real enemies of man: sin, sickness, and death. The victory had been won on the cross and through the resurrection. We fight our battles knowing that victory is sure. We are not ultimately defeated, if indeed, it is the Lord's battle and not our own that we are fighting. Our task is not to pick a fight but to live the gospel—love people into Christ and hold firm for justice in our society. If we do that, there will be conflict! Our cause may

53

never be vindicated by human approval. That's a luxury we may never enjoy. Our Scripture for today presses us beyond just believing in Christ, to serving him and suffering for him. That's where the focus should be: Christ! If we are engaged in constant communion with him, we will fight the right battles at the right time with ultimate victory secure.

> Lord, we get into so many conflicts which are of our own making. We need personal attention, control, recognition, and power. Forgive us for the times we are so busy fighting our own little battles that we miss being part of your creative battle of love for the souls of people and the structures of our society. In the quiet of this moment with you in prayer, help me to inventory my life, asking myself honestly, "Are the conflicts of my life the battle of the Lord?" Amen.

The Flavor Of Fresh Grace

STALE GRACE MAKES A SICK CHURCH.

Does your life in Christ make you strong? Does his love comfort you? Do you have fellowship with the Spirit? Do you feel compassion and love for one another? I urge you, then, make me completely happy by having the same thoughts, sharing the same love, and being one in soul and mind (Phil. 2:1, 2).

It was the person who asked the old question that made me consider an answer with new concern. He was a happy pagan who had found the joy of Christ through an authentic Christian friend. He had never had much contact with the church, and "Christian" people had never made much of an impression on him until this one friend cared for him in a costly way. Now he was told that to stay alive in his new relationship with Christ he would need to develop a daily study and prayer time and become part of some fellowship of Christians in a church. So, he started making the rounds of churches in that city. For someone who had had no contact with institutional Christianity, the experience almost shocked him out of his commitment to Christ. This is the question he asked, "Why do Christians differ on so many issues? Why can't they get it together and change this sick society? Wherever I have gone the church seems to be fussin' around about things which don't make any difference and aren't getting the good news out to people like me."

The conversation helped me to see that we accommodate ourselves to a certain level of ineffectiveness in the institutional church. With a fresh experience of Christ burning in him, the man had not found a church in his town which could share his enthusiasm about Christ.

There is a direct ratio between the flavor of fresh grace in our lives and the contagious, warm inclusiveness of our churches. There are basic spiritual laws which govern how churches come alive and stay vital: We can share only what we are continually rediscovering; we can communicate only what we are living; the gospel is not a set of ideas to be learned, but a life to be lived. As John Gardner puts it in *Self-Renewal*, "In the ever-renewing society what matures is a system or framework within which continuous innovation, renewal and rebirth can occur." [1]

Paul gives the Philippians the key to this framework for continuous renewal. Here in the opening of the second chapter, he turns his attention to their lack of unity and diminishing enthusiasm. With utmost sensitivity, he moves from what Christ has meant to him in fresh experiences of His love and in the difficulties he found in his own life to a reminder of what Christ was doing for the Philippians—and then on to what this ought to mean for their life together as a congregation. He draws them along in his thinking and then exposes the truth he wants them to discover and experience.

In a way Paul is asking, "Has Christ supported you? Has his presence strengthened you? Have you known the affection and sympathy and love of Christ?" The next question is not asked but it is there, thundering for an answer, "Do you have this kind of support, strength, and affection for one another?" What he implies is that the love with which they are to love each other is not just the work of Christ, it is Christ. The will to love in spite of differences, the desire to see and understand another, that is the Spirit. He alone can produce what Paul asks them to express: the same love, full accord, one mind. This means common love, ardor, and purpose.

These form the irreducible maximum for Christian unity. It is a gift to those who have experienced Christ's love and have the common purpose of communicating him to the lonely, sick world. Within that common purpose there is room for many different methods and points of view. Often the things which divide us have little to do with the essential purpose. They become more crucial to us than Christ and separate us from him and divide us from one another. To struggle for unity in these side issues always ends in discord. We can have compassion and understanding with people who do not share Christ or a common purpose, but not Christian unity.

Do you see what Paul has done? He has helped us to return to the basic motivation of the Christian life—Christ himself. He has enabled us to feel again the joy of that essential relationship. With the warm glow of rediscovered love, he can admonish us about the extent to which we have reproduced that love with one another. It is not that we capture that power for ourselves and then parcel it out to others, but that we love in the image of Christ because he has captured us. This creates the openness in others to receive Christ's gift for themselves.

When the institutional church grows tedious in its ecclesiastical housekeeping, it is because Christ and a vital, immediate relationship with him have been replaced by some form of orthodoxy. One church I know burns its membership roll every year and asks everyone to renew his commitment to Christ and the adventure of being part of the people of God. Everyone must publicly share what Christ means to him and why he believes that He has guided him to remain as a part of that congregation for another year. Our Lord's words to the church in Ephesus are the scriptural text for a roll burning session. "I have this against you, that you have abandoned the love you had at first. Remember then from what you have fallen, repent and do the works you did at first" (Rev. 2:4, 5, RSV).

That would be a good place for all of us to start. What about our churches? Pastors? Officers? You and me?

> Lord, today I want to repent for the bland mediocrity of my spiritual life. Paul's question in today's Scripture has forced me to realize again how much you have done for me! Help me to be a reproductive reproducer who multiplies that same love in others. I ask you to make me your agent of renewal in my church. Set our church afire, beginning with me! Amen.

When We're Boasting, We're Not Listening

WHEN CHRIST IS OUR LORD, WE DO NOT NEED
TO "LORD-IT-OVER" OTHERS.

Don't do anything from selfish ambition, or from a cheap desire to boast; but be humble toward each other, never thinking you are better than others. And look out for each other's interests, not for your own interests (Phil. 2:3, 4).

Wait a minute, Paul! Do you realize what you have asked us to do in these verses? That's not easy. In fact, in our culture, it may well be impossible.

A sure sign that the Scriptures become God's personal word to us is that they hit us where we are living. When we come to grips with what is being said, really, and grapple with what is challenged and what it would mean to live it, then we know that the Holy Spirit is at work. He has used words written long ago to cut right into our value system and character. The trouble is

57

that we can read words like our text for today and react by saying, "Isn't that nice! Wouldn't it be wonderful if people lived that way! That's just what the people in my life, my family, my church, my place of work need to hear."

But the authentic test for most of us of the presence of the Lord in our devotional meditation today would be the honest reaction, with the bold prayer: "Lord, here's a description of your style of life. But that's not how I have been conditioned to live. For me to express that quality of self-giving today would be a miracle. Your miracle in me and through me. I do most things from subtle, selfish ambition. I can camouflage it better now that I am religious, but it's willfulness at the core. You know how I drop names and accomplishments. My competition with others, even in spiritual matters, is an indication that I am not very secure in you or taking my soundings from your depth of love. I realize how little I am a "person for others." I am so often engulfed in my own interests that there is little time for the needs of others. I am quick to speak and slow to listen, anxious to impress and fearful of the demands of others. But Lord, I want to be different today! Show me what this Scripture would mean for me today if I lived it with vigor and dedication. But I can't do it without you. Live it through me today by your power!"

If we could pray the words of this Scripture that way today, it could be a beginning of a new life for us. But, it would require an incisive inventory. Paul gives us a basis for that inventory in today's Scripture.

Selfish ambition? There's nothing wrong with ambition so long as it is for a creative purpose. Selfish ambition is "thinging-it." That's using people as means to our own ends. They become things to be manipulated rather than people to be cherished and encouraged. We use them with little thought for their ultimate happiness or fulfillment. These questions demand an answer. In pressing toward my goals, to what extent do I make people rungs on my climb to accomplishment? What's happening to the people in my life?

Deep desire to boast? There's nothing wrong with healthy self-appreciation. But the problem with boasting is that we are talking and not listening. The other day I attended a meeting with a group of leaders. My expectation for a time of mutual concern and encouragement was bitterly disappointed. Everyone around the table seemed intent on impressing the others. Each marched his most recent accomplishments in the victorious Christian life before the others. The disturbing thing was that no one was listening. Each was waiting for his moment to perform on center stage and seemed impatient for his time to shine. I kept asking myself, "Why can't we listen to each other? Why aren't we rejoicing in what is happening?" That's the rub! Christ has called us to be enablers of each other to draw out the gifts and potential. Again a question, "After people are with us, do they go away impressed with how great we are or how great they can be?"

An even deeper implication is that when our insecurity stifles humility, it sprouts pretension. We fake it to make it with others. Real relationships are based on mutuality of need and openness to be Christ's love incarnate to another person.

Paul's challenge to look to the interests of others actually means, "To fix attention upon, with desire and interest in." That's no passing whim. It takes energy and involvement, time and inconvenience. But a generalized admonition becomes a great adventure if right now before this day goes any further we would dare to use our capacity of imagination to envision what we could do today which would elevate the interests of the people of our lives above our own. What could we do today which would prompt others to say in grateful appreciation, "He really knows my needs and he cares profoundly!"

Lord Christ, in the quiet of my personal prayer with you, I ask you to show me myself in my relationships. How is selfishness, self-glorification, or factionalism holding up your progress in me and my associations? Help me to write out on a piece of paper what they are and then, as an offering to you, burn the paper in affirmation that I want to be different. Then help me to write out what I would do if I truly were an enabler of people today. Amen.

How's Your Disposition?

OUR DISPOSITION IS THE OUTER MANIFESTA-
TION OF THE INNER EXPERIENCE OF CHRIST.

*The attitude [disposition] you should
have is the one that Jesus Christ had*
(Phil. 2:5).

The man leaned forward intently, "I want what my wife has found!" "What do you think she has found?" I asked. "I'm not sure; whatever it is, it has changed her disposition," he replied.

The man had come to see me because of a change in his wife. She had been a very difficult, demanding person. She had found it excruciating to be an open, giving person. Her needs kept the family up and down like a Yo-Yo. She was unpleasant when things didn't go as planned, and the demands she made on herself spilled over in dissatisfaction with her husband and children.

A group of women in our church invited her to become a part of an Enabler's Group in her neighborhood. The women met to have coffee, study the Bible, share mutual concerns, and pray for each other. In these women and their gracious relationships, this man's wife had found what Christ could do to love and liberate a person. One day at the end of a meeting she stayed on to talk with one of the women about her life and what she was doing to the people around her. The reaction of her children and her disintegrating marriage had convinced her that she must do something about her rotten disposition. She began her relationship with Christ with an experiment: "Christ, if you are alive as these people say you are, help me to change my disposition."

The result of that prayer came slowly but inevitably. She repeated the prayer every day and in each situation in which she was tempted to blast off with vitriolic consternation.

It was some months later that her husband came to see me. He wanted the same change for himself. She had not preached or pressed her faith on him. Instead, she had simply asked Christ to manifest his character in and through her. The change was too remarkable for him to resist.

"What would you say is the distinguishing mark of a Christian?" someone asks. I think it is his disposition. Not just his beliefs or ideas or words, but his disposition. By disposition I mean more than countenance or facial expression; it is the inner quality of life which expresses itself in attitudes, actions, and awareness. It is the outer expression of the integration of thought, feelings, and will around a unifying motive.

Paul challenged the Philippians to have the same mind that was in Christ Jesus. He was referring here to more than thought or developed theories. A disposition of mind—one of the many ways Paul describes the indwelling of Christ in our lives.

The same thought is communicated to the Colossians when Paul describes the source of Christian character: "To them God chose to make known how great among the Gentiles are the riches of the glory of this mystery, which is Christ in you, the hope of glory" (Col. 1:27, RSV).

Here in Philippians Paul has pleaded for unity and oneness in Christ. He uses disposition as a synonym for the Spirit living in us. The quality of humility, self-giving, and interest in the welfare of others is possible only as a result of the remolding of our disposition around the character of Christ.

The secret of discovering this is not to try to be more loving to please our Lord. Many of us were taught that we should make an effort to honor Christ by reproducing Christian characteristics to win his affirmation. These Paul clearly delineates as the fruit of Christ's Spirit in us. In Galatians 5 he listed the elements of Christian disposition: love, joy, peace, patience, kindness, goodness, faithfulness, gentleness, self-control. Without root there can be no fruit. And our Lord put it bluntly, "Abide in me, and I in you. As the branch cannot bear fruit by itself, unless it abides in the vine, neither can you, unless you abide in me . . . for apart from me you can do nothing" (John 15: 4, 5, RSV).

Who in your life would want to find Christ because of your disposition?

Lord, I want to talk to you about my disposition. Help me to get outside of myself enough today to see the projection of my personality to others. Change my disposition, remold me around the dominant desire to express the fruit of the Spirit today. I consciously give myself to abide in you. Give me the courage to honestly review how much of your disposition has become mine today. It's going to be a great day, and I thank you in advance for it. Amen.

Empty The Cup!

SELF-EMPTYING IS SELF-FULFILLMENT.

He always had the very nature of God, but he did not think that by force he should try to become equal with God. Instead, of his own free will he gave it all up, and took the nature of a servant. He was born like man, he appeared in human likeness (Phil. 2:6, 7).

"This is the Body of the Lord Jesus, broken for you and I am willing to be broken upon for you. This is the cup of the new covenant in Christ's blood making a new relationship between us. As Christ was poured out for us, I am willing to have my life poured out for you."

These are the words the elders said to each other as they broke the bread and passed the cup in a very moving Communion service at the conclusion of a retreat. In expressing these dynamic words of institution they captured the meaning of being a self-emptying fellowship.

The charter for the self-emptying church is here in Philippians 2:5-11 which will be the center of our attention these next few days. It is known as the *Kenosis* passage. Kenosis is the Greek word meaning "to empty," and proclaims the nature of the self-emptying humility of the Son of God as he became incarnate in humanity. The true meaning of the disposition we talked about yesterday is delineated dramatically for us. Every time I study this passage I am moved with inexpressible emotion. It breaks me open to deep levels of praise and thanksgiving which I can hardly contain and to a new attitude toward God, my life, and my relationships. Here is both motive and method of the Christian life. What those elders said to each other and are seeking to live out in this life together is an extension of the incarnation. Jesus gave himself totally for us. That's the way we are to live with each other!

". . . though he was in the form of God, did not count equality with God a thing to be grasped, but emptied himself, taking the form of a servant, being born in the likeness of men" (Phil. 2:6-8, RSV). There are two words the Greeks used for "form." One means essential nature; the other, outward manifestation. Here Paul used the first to describe Christ. He is the essence of God and became God among men in the incarnation. Christ didn't have to grasp this (actually means snatch, clutch, or steal) because it was his already as essential, unalterable God. Instead, he emptied himself utterly of divine aloofness and poured himself into our humanity. He actually became one of us! Again the same word is used for "form." He became the essence of a servant, "being born in the likeness of men." He felt what we feel, suffered what we suffer as he emptied himself of deity to assume humanity. Christ was not pretending or playing a part. He revealed to us what life was created to be in self-giving, person-centric, sacrificial love.

The seeming paradox of Jesus being God and man is confusing only from our point of view when we reason back from the man Jesus to God. Begin with God and trace the magnificent movement of his self-emptying love through the incarnation, death, resurrection, and back to eternal glory. That makes the difference! Christ was not just a human being but eternal God, and what he is now to us in daily living is focused in what he has revealed in Jesus of Nazareth. That self-emptying is the same way he wants to live his life through us as our disposition.

Empty your cup and it will always be full. Break yourself open and you will become whole!

> Lord God, thank you for coming in Jesus Christ so that I could know who you are and what I was meant to be. Let my heart be broken by the things which break your heart. Remind me that at the end of this day I will have only the things I have given away. Amen.

End Run Around Golgotha

THE CROSS IS THEN AND NOW.

He was humble and walked the path of obedience to death—his death on the cross (Phil. 2:8).

"Don't try to sneak around Golgotha!"

I shall never forget these words spoken by Thomas Torrence to a class at Edinburgh. The temptation to ignore the cross in an understanding of God or in the living of life is always beguiling. At the foot of the cross we are forced to see things as they are.

H. H. Farmer's words in *The World and God* put it undeniably, "The darkness of man's mind must be broken through so that we can begin to see things as they really are . . . God as He really is, Himself as He really is. The saving revelation must be such that at the same time it shows man the truth and makes it possible for him to be sincere with it." [2]

That's just what happened on the cross! The cross was in God's essential nature before it was displayed on Golgotha. It was not an afterthought, a result of circumstances, or an expression of the worst that the anger and hostility of men could do. God being who he is and man being what he is, it could not have been different.

Our end run around Golgotha is caused by an unwillingness to admit we need something that drastic to save us from our self-centeredness. Often our liturgical and symbolic use of the cross is a way of faithless familiarity. The sharp truth is blunted by our flippant assumption of what must be experienced anew each day. The question which must be answered every day is: "If I had been the only person alive would the cross have been necessary?"

What God revealed of his forgiving nature on the cross is still his attitude toward us. That's why the cross is the center of our faith in every age and in every day of our lives. The Christian life begins and is renewed at the cross. We know that the cross revealed the way God loved from the beginning. But there in time and space, in "human form," God revealed his forgiving love. Nothing can ever be the same after Golgotha—the once, never to be repeated sacrifice for our sins. God has closed the door on man's efforts to be good enough through religion, or self-effort. The cross was a decisive act of canceling man's sin and opening of a new age of gracious acceptance.

The cross was then and now. If it was not then, it cannot be now. But if it is not now as a radical rediscovery, what it was then is robbed of its liberating power.

We too have a cross. I don't mean the sloppy sentimentalism which identifies some difficult situation, burdens, or a person as a "cross" we have to bear. The cross was the result of Jesus' obedience, as today's Scripture reminds us. The same is true for us. It means death to self-generated, self-centered plans and images. The cross means obedience to seek and do God's will in all our responsibilities and relationships.

Oswald Chambers picks up this same thought and clarifies what our Lord is trying to do in us today: "The words of the Lord hurt and offend until there is nothing left to hurt or offend. Jesus Christ has no tenderness whatever toward anything that is ultimately going to ruin a man in the service of God. Our Lord's answers are not based on caprice, but on the knowledge of what is in a man. If the Spirit of God brings to your mind a word of the Lord that hurts you, you may be sure that there is something He wants to hurt to death." [3]

> Gracious Lord, thank you for what you did for me on the cross. I long for that cross to become real to me again today. I accept again your forgiving love and ask for the courage to become obedient in doing your will in my life. I give myself to rediscover and experience the cross as the central reality of my life. Amen.

A Trumpet Blast To Fire Our Blood

IF YOUR KNEES ARE SHAKING, KNEEL ON THEM!

For this reason God raised him to the highest place above, and gave him the name that is greater than any other name, so that all beings in heaven, and on earth, and in the world below will fall on their knees, in honor of the name of Jesus (Phil. 2:9, 10).

One of my favorite quotations is from John Arthur Gossip: "If we would help people to be valiant in their Christian living, we should be ringing out over the world that Christ has won, that evil is toppling, that the end is sure, that nothing can for long resist our mighty and victorious Lord. That is the tonic that we need to keep us healthy, the trumpet blast to fire our blood, and send us crowding in behind the Master, swinging happily upon our way, ready and eager to face anything, laughing and singing and recklessly unafraid, because the feel of victory is in the air, as our hearts thrill to it." [4]

That's exactly what I think Paul is trying to do for the Philippians, and for us. The dramatic, doxological language of our Lord's exultation puts fire in our being. But don't miss the inner intention. Paul wanted his readers to feel both the humiliation and consequent exultation of Christ. His affirmation of Christ's voluntary act of humility, self-renunciation and consequent exultation was not only adoration but admonition. What he implies is that if the Philippians give up their practice of self-aggrandizement and prefer one another in love, God will raise them up and defend their cause. Remember the context: This is the description of Christ's disposition. It was so they might "have in them the disposition which was in Christ." Romans 6 leaps into our minds. "What shall we say then? Are we to continue in sin that grace may abound? By no means! How can we who died to sin still live in it? Do you not know that all of us who have been baptized into Christ Jesus were baptized into his death? We were buried therefore with him by baptism into death, so that as Christ was raised from the dead by the glory of the Father, we too might walk in newness of life. For if we have been united with him in a death like his, we shall certainly be united with him in a resurrection like his" (6:1-5, RSV).

This leaves us with a challenge for today. Our responsibility is obedience; God's response is exultation. Resurrection is God's answer to the worst that life dishes out. We are raised with Christ when we begin the new life that is eternal fellowship with him. Death is defeated and no longer a fear. Daily resurrection happens when Christ brings good out of the worst circumstances. We can dare to say with Shelley, "If winter comes, can spring be far behind?"

John Orran said, "Without a trust that God has a purpose He can make sure, human cruelty dethrones for us either God's goodness or His omnipotence; and one is a mockery without the other." Paul has helped us to regain our perspective of God's power to say the final word in the glorification of Christ. The cross will reoccur each day in our lives, but so will resurrection.

What amazing freedom that gives us for today. We don't need to defend, boost, or glorify ourselves. Leave that to God.

The other day I learned what that means. I had experienced some excruciating frustration in trying to lead a committee for which I am responsible. My own ego had become entangled in the machinery of institutional religion. Only after I gave up my willful determination did I feel the release of God's inner liberation. "That group belongs to me," he said, "I will do with it as I will . . . and it will be more wonderful than you could have imagined." The load was lifted!

> Gracious Lord of new beginnings, help me to surrender my need to exalt myself. Help me to focus my life on an exalted Lord and know that you will bring your perfect plan out of the entangled mesh of my own scheming. I trust you, Lord, today. Amen.

The Secret Of Power

THE "NAME" WHICH UNLOCKS THE POWER
OF GOD IS JESUS CHRIST OUR LORD.

And every tongue confess that Jesus Christ is Lord, to the glory of God the Father (Phil. 2:11, RSV).

A Muslim who has been attending the services of a church I served had a miraculous healing of pain in his back while sitting in the sanctuary during worship. Later he came to me to understand what had happened.

"I want to find this God who has healed my back, but I find it difficult because of my background to believe that Jesus was more than a prophet."

I asked him if he would believe what the God who healed him had said about himself. He agreed to try but was hung up on whether Jesus was any more divine than Mohammed or Moses. Subsequently, in frequent visits we talked more about the God who revealed himself in Jesus than about Jesus who revealed God. That shifted the conversation into seeing Jesus as divine exposure, not just as one of the best of good men. Then we could see the incarnation as God graciously saying to him, "I love you, understand all your needs, and will give you a new life if you will trust me." My friend's response was, "How can I know him?"

In that light, we could talk about Jesus as Lord. God has called us to himself in Christ. Our response is to make him, the eternal God of all creation and the Father of all men, whom we have come to know in Christ, the Lord of our lives. That means response, trust, and surrender of all we have and are—which is enabled by God's own gift of faith. Our task is to receive. This man did just that and asked to be baptized in outward recognition of the fact that he had turned the leadership of his life over to God whom he now knows by the name of Lord. Like all of us, he still has much to discover and many problems to be solved, but he's on the way.

I believe that the greatest need of the church in America is to rediscover this basic creed of the early church: Jesus is Lord. The missing ingredient is the will. It is possible to rationalize the existence and power of Christ without relationalizing his Lordship and experiencing his power. The commitment of the will unlocks the joy and adventure of following Christ. It means that we seek out his will, determine his priorities for us, and make the hard choices of faithful obedience. To join with the great company of heaven and earth to "openly proclaim that Jesus Christ is Lord" is to fulfill our destiny in creation.

Renewal takes place in a church when people who have rejoiced in their Savior are released by their Lord. This means the discovery of his presence and purpose for every facet of life. The bold new apostolate of hope God is raising up in our day is made up of people who are excited about their faith because of fresh experiences of the Lord at work in the realities of daily life. He has become the intervening, interacting, indwelling Lord of their marriages, struggles with identity, problems of vocation, tensions of relationships, and fears of failure.

I'll never forget the exclamation of a Presbyterian layman in a church I visited, "We've been talking about Jesus Christ around here for years. But when you stood up and said, 'The Living Lord is here. Let the people say Amen,' I was too flabbergasted to respond. I had never heard that before."

Kierkegaard was not overstating the case when he said, "Christendom has done away with Christianity, without being quite aware of it. The consequence is that, if anything is to be done about it, one must try again to introduce Christianity to Christendom."

The name that is greater than any other name is Jesus Christ our Lord. That's the theme of this majestic passage in Philippians we have been considering these past few days. "The Name" is a Hebrew title denoting office, rank, dignity, and exultation. It refers to power and authority. Through the "name" of Jesus our Lord we have direct access to the limitless power of God. The same power which raised him from the dead is available to us.

Two mind-expanding, consciousness-elevating, mood-liberating statements of our Lord set the expectation and hope for today: "If you abide in me, and my words abide in you, ask what you will, and it shall be done for you" (John 15:7, RSV). "These things which I have done you shall do also, and greater things than these shall you do for I go to the Father" (John 14:12, RSV).

Lord, our question is not which religion. You know how inadequate they all are, but to listen to what you have said about yourself in Jesus. Give us the gift of faith to make you Lord of our lives. If I have done it before, I do it now again in complete trust that I belong to you. If I have never done it, make this the day of my birth. Lord, "I believe, help Thou my unbelief." I give myself completely—mind, emotions, and will. Amen.

LOVE AS CHRIST HAS LOVED THE CHURCH;
FOLLOW AS IF FOLLOWING HIM.

*So then, my friends, as you always
obeyed me when I was with you, it is
even more important that you obey me
now, while I am away from you* (Phil.
2:12).

Do you ever have difficulty getting people to do what you want? Is it a challenge to you to give people direction with any assurance that they will follow? Do you ever wish you had some kind of power over your family or friends so that they would do what you say just because you have asked it?

All of us have responsibilities of leadership in some areas—in our homes, among our friends, or in some professional capacity. How would you like to be able to say what Paul said to the Philippians about obeying him? Ever want to say that to your spouse, children, or friends? We don't use that word much any more, do we? It has been taken out of the marriage service, our obligations to employers are carefully delineated in labor-management agreements, and we resist authority on most levels of our society. Obedience is always a quid pro quo commodity which we barter for something we need: safety, salary, support, approval. But even here we can bolt the scene and quit—leave home or break a relationship.

Yet, we all need leadership on some level of our lives. And any leader needs support whether he is a parent, an office manager, or a club president. Group leadership where everyone is equally in charge often ends in anarchy. Most of the advocates of that idea whom I have known have usually wanted to get free of a strong leader, and their advocacy for everyone leading often ends in their being in charge.

Paul gives us the key of great leadership. Before he asks the Philippians to obey, he refers to them as "dear friends." Actually, the Greek text means "beloved ones." The word refers to the love that God is. This is the love which is a gift of the Holy Spirit, which motivates sacrificial love of one's self for others. Paul had demonstrated this love for the Philippians in concrete ways. He could ask them to obey because he had their confidence and trust.

This leaves me with some penetrating questions. Think of the people of your life.

1. Do we love the people we lead?
2. Do they know it?
3. What tangible evidence of our caring for them as persons has been vividly displayed and enacted and verbalized this past week?
4. Do they know that we will their ultimate good?
5. Do they share in formulating the direction we give them? People can only support what they share in developing.
6. Have we enabled them to set realizable goals for themselves which we help them inventory consistently?
7. Do we stand with them in costly involvement?
8. Are we vulnerable enough to admit our own failures so that an ambience of grace is communicated?

The other side of this Scripture for today is a challenge to consider what kind of follower we are. Openness to the thought and insight and direction of another is a sure sign of maturity. But, the people of God, both biblically and historically, have not excelled in a capacity to follow their appointed, installed, or ordained leaders.

I like the question which was used at one time in the installation of elders in the church, "Will you the members of this congregation follow these elders in so far as they follow Christ?"

Congregations across the nation need to give loyalty and support to those whom they have elected to lead, and I hold as sacred the Holy Spirit-guided decisions of those leaders. We can move no faster nor further than they have discerned the direction. This leaves me with some questions about being an obedient follower:

1. Do we pray for the people who are responsible for leadership over us?

2. When is the last time we prayed for the elders or leaders of our church, one by one, by name?

3. Do we communicate our support of the people who lead us in all areas of life?

4. Are we willing to contribute to the process of understanding a direction?

5. Are we willing to support a decision once it's made and not saw sawdust?

6. Are we willing to say nothing about a leader which we have not first said to him face to face?

7. Do we give our leaders the freedom to fail and the grace to begin again?

In Paul's description of marriage in the fifth chapter of Ephesians, there is a mutuality hinted at which we often miss. He says, "Husbands, love your wives as Christ has loved the church." Then he says, "Wives, be obedient to your husbands as unto the Lord." Rather than simply categorizing these qualities as pertaining to each sex, why not consider them as the responsibility of both husbands and wives? In fact, a profound challenge is here for all of us in every relationship. What if we all, at home, in the church, or in our social life loved people "as Christ loved the church and gave himself for her"? In the same context, what would happen if we were open to follow, listen to, share with each other the obedience we would have if we were reacting to Christ himself?

Try that one on for size . . . today!

Lord Jesus, I want to be the kind of leader you have shown me in your own ministry. Help me to be willing to follow your leading through others. I want to be the kind of person who loves as you loved the church and obey in my responsibilities as if I were honoring you. Amen.

Sleeping Between The Lightning And The Thunder

A GIFT IS NEVER RECEIVED UNTIL IT IS USED.

Keep on working, with fear and trembling, to complete your salvation (Phil. 2:12). *Work out your own salvation with fear and trembling* (Phil. 2:12, RSV). *The fear of the Lord is the beginning of knowledge; fools despise wisdom and instruction* (Prov. 1:7, RSV).

William Irwin Thompson gives us a remarkable image in his fascinating book *At the Edge of History.* "The future is beyond knowing, but the present is beyond belief. We make so much noise with technology that we cannot discover that the stargate is in our foreheads. But the time has come, the revelation has occurred, and the guardian seers have seen the lightning strike the darkness we call reality and now we sleep in the brief interval between the lightning and the thunder." [5]

Asleep between the lightning and the thunder This vivid picture, from a Christian's point of view, portrays not only what has happened to our civilization but what has happened to many of us in our growth as Christians. Let us interpret it this way. Between the lightning of God's revelation of his love for us in Christ at the beginning of our Christian experience and the thunder of our physical death, we are tempted to be somnolent saints. A little boy was asked why he fell out of bed one night. He explained, "I fell asleep too close to where I got in." That sounds like what happens to a lot of us in our Christian life. Staying awake between the lightning and the thunder means going on in new discoveries of the implications of Christ's lordship for every relationship, plan, expenditure, vision, hope, or dream. Once we turn our lives over to him, he begins to disturb and unsettle every area of life. Christ is not concerned for our comfort as much as he is about our character. Salvation is a gift, as we will stress particularly in tomorrow's meditation, but it can be frustrated by our resistance to God's remedial, disquieting reformation of our nature.

Paul challenged the Philippians to work out their salvation with fear and trembling. I think he meant that the awesome realization of the possibility of being unfaithful to our potential in Christ is the creative source of going on to maturity in Christ. He did not mean that we are to devise our own plan of salvation. Nor did he mean that we were to develop a method of working our way into a right relationship with God by our own efforts. And it certainly does not mean that we are to work out what God has worked in, as many interpreters have suggested.

The word for "worked out" is a verb which means to bring to full and complete conclusion. What this suggests is that we are to continue to grow in the realization of God's love and strategy for us. This we do with the recognition that we could misuse our freedom and resist God's Spirit. We can lose any faculty we refuse to use. The sin against the Holy Spirit is the sin of so often and so consistently refusing God's will that in the end it cannot be recognized when it comes even fully displayed. Elsewhere Paul warned against grieving and resisting the Spirit. He reminded Timothy, "Do not neglect the gift you have," and "Rekindle the gift of God that is in you."

There is a real difference between being afraid of God and having the fear of the Lord. Many people feel that if they offend God he will punish them with reciprocal judgment. Others live in anguish, waiting for some terrible thing to happen to settle the accounts of heaven for their failures.

The author of Proverbs said that the fear of the Lord is the beginning of wisdom. This means a balanced combination of awe, wonder, and humility. It comes from the experience of the power and majesty of God. When we are confronted with the beauty of the natural world; when we see God's face in the love of another person; when we experience a serendipity of grace in an impossible situation and know that God has stepped in for our good; then we are filled with awesome, creative fear that makes us different as we handle the gift of life.

This is the kind of fear and trembling Paul is talking about with the Philippians. They had been entrusted with the answer to human futility and anguish. How easily it could become mundane, bland, and urbane. They could miss the joy of it all and block God's Spirit in them. Think of the ways we frustrate God's plan for us. Consider what the arrogance of trying to live on our own resources does to us and the people around us. What about our feverish efforts to stuff our lives with so much activity that there is no time left to ask God what he wants us to do? That is cause for fear and trembling, isn't it? Obedience to our Lord is the continuous new beginning of unpredictable possibilities.

A woman recently exclaimed, "What you're asking me to do is go back to years ago and pick up where I tucked Christ into a convenient pocket of my life. That won't be easy. Do you realize what you are suggesting?" I reassured her I did. The alternative to reordering her priorities was to go back to sleep and wait for the thunder!

> Lord, thank you for the gift of knowing and loving you; yet all of the possibilities you give me can be limited by my unwillingness. Thank you for the creative fear of not grasping the full potential of life. I long to have the kind of faith which surrenders all I am in faithfulness—not guilty fear—and issues in a consuming passion to taste all of the potentials you have put in our grasp. In awe and wonder, I want to grow in Christ today. Amen.

Let God Love You!

OURS IS TO BE WILLING. THE REST IS UP TO GOD.

For God is always at work in you to
make you willing and able to obey his
own purpose (Phil. 2:13).

I could hardly believe it was the same man! When I first met him he was tense and impatient. As a Presbyterian clergyman, he was as starchy as his stiff clerical collar and tabs. His congregation was the length and shadow of his own stern efforts to be adequate for God. Everything about the church was suffocatingly proper. The stained glass windows, the impeccable Gothic architecture, the lovely organ music, and the classical rhetoric blended together in the symmetry of a religious institution. But joy was missing. The people did not seem to be enjoying either God or each other.

My next visit was so surprisingly different it baffled me. The people were warm and gracious. And the worship had a ring of reality and adventuresomeness of Christianity as a life to be lived and not a set of principles to be observed. When I visited with the church leaders, I was aware of a permeating love and closeness among them.

What had made the difference? The building had not been remodeled, the hymns were the same, and the order of worship had only changed slightly. The same people were there but they were not the same!

Something had happened to that pastor and then to his leaders, and it had spread throughout the church. He had attended a conference which had dealt with how to cooperate with God. The conference theme was, "To love God is to let God love you." The content had dealt with how to work cooperatively with God's Spirit in us to meet our basic needs and to enable us to discover our hidden potential as the people of God. In the personal small groups which met after each content session, my friend had discovered that it was okay to admit his needs and to begin to envision what God could do in him and through him if he dared to open himself and his relationships. He had always felt constrained to show himself as strong. People had been attracted to him as a person, and the burden of carrying that responsibility was overwhelming. During that conference week, he dared to let God love him. When he returned home, he was free to share what had happened. He began to talk about what God was doing in his own life. And he allowed people to know him and become a vital part of a genuine renewal which spread through his church.

The formula for cooperating with God is this: To love God is to let God love you; to let God love you is to be completely open to what he wants to do in every part of your thinking, feeling, and attitude.

That's what I believe Paul is talking about in today's Scripture. In it he says some magnificent things about God and some motivating things about us. God is always at work in us. He chose us, loved us, and gave us the gift of faith to respond. He persists in us and will not let us rest at any stage of growth. Paul said it clearly, "For by grace you have been saved through faith; and this is not your own doing, it is a gift of God—not because of works, lest any man should boast. For we are his workmanship, created in Christ Jesus for good works, which God prepared beforehand, that we should walk in them" (Eph. 2:8–10, RSV). God knows what he is doing with us. Even the desire to want what he wants is a gift. We can trust him at every point, in the difficulties and the delights of life, because he will weave them into his ultimate plan to make us like his Son and prepare us to live with him forever. So we can relax and enjoy the journey! God will not leave us unfinished or incomplete. Therefore, we can enter into each new day with the confidence that he will make us willing to be willing to do his will.

Cooperating with God is threefold: discovering where we need to grow; being open to being changed; and receiving his power to act. Here are some questions which I find helpful in discerning how.

What's the thing in me which makes it most difficult to be open to Christ today?

Where have I grown recently and where do I most need to grow in personality, relationships, and responsibilities?

If I could see things from God's point of view, what would I want most to change?

78

If I were not hemmed in by caution and reserve, what would I do or say today as an expression of Christ's love?

To ask these questions is a sign that God's work of giving us willingness is well on the way. Our Scripture tells us that a further part of God's work is to make us able. He will give us the power to act on the agenda which the answers to these questions have written. That's cooperation! So, why not let God love you?

> Thank you, Lord, that you are even now making me willing to be willing to grow. You are at work in me, unsettling my complacency and blasting me open to grow as a person. Help me to cooperate with you. Amen.

Hope To Displace Despair

WHAT ABOUT YOUR LIFE IN CHRIST WOULD
MAKE OTHERS ACUTELY AWARE THAT THEY
ARE MISSING SOMETHING . . . SOMEONE?

> *Do everything without complaining or arguing, that you may be innocent and pure, God's perfect children who live in a world of crooked and mean people. You must shine among them like stars lighting up the sky, as you offer them the message of life* (Phil. 2:14–16).

There is a new distrust of words, speechmaking, and theorizing which pervades our time. Our despair today is expressed in the demise of innocent trust in what people say. A man's word is no longer sacred. Cynicism, criticism, and complaining pollute the atmosphere. Our nation longs to hope again and yet the diminutive gods in which we have placed our hope in culture, institutions, and government have fallen from the thrones of inerrancy.

What a great day to be the church! It could be the greatest day for centuries to write the next chapter in the Book of Acts. We stand a chance of moving from being an extension of our culture to being its hope.

But a very different kind of church must emerge in America. Barth said that the church is to be a provisional demonstration of the Kingdom of God. The Kingdom of God means the rule of God. I believe the church is about to have its finest hour in America. But only as it is different from our culture—offering a quality of life which can be found nowhere else—can we survive as something more than a custom in folk religion. Paul's question to the Corinthian church leaps out of our New Testament, "Who sees anything different in you?" Or as the Jewish philosopher Martin Buber bruises us, "If the Messiah has come, where are the Messiah's people?"

The Scripture from Philippians we read today could have been written to the church in America. Paul takes his agenda for the Philippian church from the kind of world in which it existed. He reasoned back from purpose to program. What the church should be is inseparably related to what its members should do in the world. And what a purpose he gives them: Shine as lights in the darkness . . . offer the message of life.

"Put it to us straight, Doctor, is he going to live?" This is the question with which we confronted a physician who had just come from the emergency ward where he was treating a friend. His answer was one I will never forget. "Well, the lab reports tell us that he is a very sick man, at the point of death. But I'm not just watching lab reports, I'm ministering to a man."

He continued to work with our friend for hours with that wonderful combination of faith and medical knowledge and skill. Finally, he told us that he was out of danger and would get well.

We are often tempted to pay too much attention to the lab reports about the spiritual condition of people and our world and give up hope. If we read only the analysis of our generation in news magazines and commentaries, we would be tempted to despair. Also, if all we see is the outer wrappings of people in what Paul called a perverse and crooked generation (means distorted, having a twist), we will never get on with our purpose—to offer the message of life. Often the lab reports are so bad about our world that we see problems instead of seizing opportunities. People's actions put us off so that we cannot see them as sick people in desperate need of the word of life. Underneath the most hardened bitterness or the most highly polished sophistication we will discover in the selfish, proud, negative, or blasé, a need for love, harmony, solidarity, trust, forgiveness, and some assurance about death: a love which is far greater than the facsimiles offered by the world. This is a thirst which the activities and possessions, or even the satisfactions of earth cannot quench. As Orgo Betti put it, "Each of these mysterious needs is one side of a perimeter whose complete figure, when we finally perceive it, has one name: God." And our calling is to offer the word of life in Jesus Christ and stay with the patient until he is out of danger.

The tiny little colony of Christians at Philippi had to struggle for its life in an overwhelming sea of paganism. To survive as a unique entity was not easy. That's why Paul is so decisive in his corrective about their life together. Their culture was in a death-grip of dissatisfaction and discord. He wanted their fellowship to be a dramatic difference for Philippi to see. He knew that the world could not be saved by talk, not even eloquent rhetoric of perfect ideals. People could not be changed by their reasoning, however persuasive, unless their lives were a persuasion. Sinful Philippi would not be changed by advice except as that advice was lived before the words were spoken. The city had more religions than could be counted. The new life in Christ must therefore be conveyed through changed human personalities. That's the power of the incarnation: power through personality.

Therefore, complaining and arguing were luxuries they could

ill afford. The words are very vivid in the Greek. The first means to "mutter and murmur" and refers not to loud, outspoken dissatisfaction, but to an undercurrent of debilitating discord. By arguing, Paul means more than healthy intellectual debate, but questioning another person's integrity with suspicion or doubt.

Paul urges the church to be innocent and pure. Ah! There's the difference the church has to offer. The same problems which are in the world are also in the church. But how we handle them is our witness to the world. The way is in Paul's admonition that they should be innocent and pure. That means unmixed, unadulterated, guileless. Honesty, openness, and straightforwardness enable Christians to handle their differences. Only what's hidden can hurt the fellowship. Open sharing, mutual forgiveness and submission of conflicts to God's light in prayer will keep the church healthy and strong. Fosdick said, "All public consequences go back to secret conflicts. . . . We are deceived by the garish stage-setting of big scenes in history. . . . The decisive battles of the world are hidden, and all the outward conflicts are but the echo and reverberation of the more real and inward war. . . . Prayer is the fight for the power to see and the courage to do the will of God." [6]

I look for a great swing back to the church in America in the last half of the seventies. It's the only hope for our culture. So let's not try to mirror our culture but model the amazing difference Christ can make in us and our relationships.

If we are to shine like stars in the night let's dare to believe that it will be a morning star. That's the last star which is seen just before dawn, heralding the beginning of a new day.

> Lord Jesus, Light of the world. You have elected me to be a light in the world. I pray to be the kind of open, honest, illuminated person who has nothing to hide, and hope to give. I pray for a quality of life in our church which will astound the world around us with the difference a life totally open to you and each other can mean. Amen.

A Liberating Libation

WHAT WOULD IT MEAN TO LIVE SACRIFI-
CIALLY . . . REALLY? WHAT WOULD IT
MEAN TO AFFIRM OTHERS WHO DARE TO BE
OBEDIENT TO THE MASTER?

*Perhaps my life's blood is to be poured
out like an offering on the sacrifice that
your faith offers to God. If that is so, I
am glad, and share my joy with you all.
In the same way, you too must be glad
and share your joy with me* (Phil. 2:17–
18).

I have an imp in me. I must keep him under control because
there are times in religious ceremonies when I want to interrupt
the unexamined language of hymns and ritual and say, "Hey,
did you hear what you just said or sang?"

The other day I participated in the corporate sin of un-
reality in a worship service where I was guest preacher. With
gusto and unmeditated enthusiasm the congregation sang, "Take
my silver and my gold not a mite would I withhold."

As I looked over the beautifully dressed congregation, the
inner imp said, "Oh yeah?"

The pastor received the offering and prayed, "This offering,
Oh Lord, is symbolic of our sacrificial lives poured out as an
offering for your sacrifice for us all."

The end of my tongue hurt because I had to bite it to keep
from saying what I was feeling. Next, the host pastor introduced
me by saying, "At great sacrifice to his schedule, our speaker
has come to us today."

My imp responded inside, "If that's all you ever sacrifice,
you've gotten off easy!"

The service ended with a triumphant crescendo of egregious
language in the words of the closing hymn:

"Jesus, I my cross have taken, all to leave and follow Thee,
Destitute, despised, forsaken, Thou from hence my all shall be;
Perish every fond ambition, all I've sought, or hoped, or known;
Yet how rich is my condition, God and heaven are still my own."

We certainly sing and pray and preach beyond where we're living, don't we? "What are six things you have denied yourself this past week because of what you believe? On the positive side what evidence of sacrificial living would anyone observe in you?" My imp asked me the question . . . so I thought I would share the discomfort with you!

Paul and the Philippians had sacrificial living in common. They had suffered for what they believed. Paul had been persecuted in every imaginable way. Eventually he died a martyr's death because of Jesus Christ. The Philippians were persecuted with social rejection and suffered physically for what they believed. The church was under political attack and the hostility Paul experienced when he was with them had been turned on them with indefatigable persistence.

In today's passage Paul pictures himself and his death as a libation poured out on the sacrifice of the Philippians' faith offered to God. This was not religious hyperbole; it was realistic honesty. To be a Christian was dangerous and costly. That's why the images taken from the sacrificial language of the time are so crucial. A libation was a cup of wine poured out on a sacrificial offering in the religious ceremonies of that time.

What a twist! In Paul's day people sacrificed animals symbolic of the sacrifice of their own lives for the gods. The offering was for atonement or vicarious suffering. Today we sacrifice words of faithfulness as a substitute for sacrificial living. If we pray and sing about it long enough, we soon begin to think of ourselves as really living as contemporary martyrs for our faith.

What would it mean to be sacrificial today? Watch out for the dangers of self-generated, self-appointed sacrifice! There is an abundance of guilt-oriented prophetic admonition about that today.

The only way I have ever been able to deal with this passage meaningfully is to couple it with Romans 12:1, "So then, my brothers, because of God's many mercies to us, I make this appeal to you: Offer yourselves as a living sacrifice to God, dedicated to his service and pleasing to him." The Greek word for "bodies" as it is used here means the totality of our lives, our commitments, loyalties, and involvements. We are to give our whole self to Christ.

Our task is not to define the terms of our sacrifice for Christ. Faithfulness to him clarifies the form and gives the force of our discipleship. What is sacrificial for one of us may require little of another. Our Lord is the focus. We are to keep our eyes on him, not what others are doing.

I am sure that we are holding a live wire in today's Scripture. It jars us with the realization of how little our faith costs us. But an orgy of paranoid masochism will help no one. A creative urgency to get on with obedient times with our Lord and faithful following of his marching orders will get us into sacrifice soon enough.

Paul wanted to affirm the Philippians in their troubles. Their suffering was validated by the joy they experienced out of the profound realization of grace in their difficulties. Joy is always the outward manifestation of the inward experience of God's unchanging, gracious love. The joy Paul shared with the Philippians was no easy happiness, but a result of the endurance of painful problems through the sustaining power of grace.

This passage leaves us with two questions: "Where in my life is Christ calling me to give up my security, safety, and comfort to be offered up on the altar of the needs of people and our world?" and, "How can I be a libation to encourage and affirm this quality of giving in others?"

We can be a libation of affirmation and encouragement to help each other know it's all worthwhile because Christ has won the victory for us. We do not need to repeat Golgotha, but to incarnate its implications. That will mean sacrifice, but it will be according to the guidance and direction of our Lord.

Gracious Lord, I get uneasy when I talk beyond where I am living. I don't want to play church. But rather than water down the great Scriptures and hymns of challenge to my level of blandness, Lord, give me courage to be faithful today, to be obedient to your guidance. I surrender my life—gifts, time, talents, convenience, schedule, and resources to be used by you as you wish today. Help me to be as ready to act as I was to say that. Make me a credible Christian today, Lord. Amen.

Say It!   Say It!

SEVEN WORDS WHICH COULD CHANGE OUR LIFE ARE "GOD LOVES YOU AND SO DO I!"

I hope in the Lord Jesus to send Timothy to you soon, so that I may be cheered by news of you. I have no one like him, who will be genuinely anxious for your welfare (Phil. 2:19–20, RSV).

I remember comforting a good friend at the time of his wife's death some years ago. He stood by the graveside weeping. We looked at each other intently. I saw the grief of his tearstained face:

"There was so much left unsaid."

"There was so much that I had planned to do to express my love."

"Do you think she knew? I found it very difficult to put into words and action how I felt about her! But it's too late."

A father said much the same thing about his son who had died unexpectedly:

"I used to complain about the expenses for that boy. How I wish I could give him something, someone, myself! Right now. If I only had him back!"

Carlyle's wife, Jane Welsh, was often a disturbance and a bore to him, and he treated her badly. But after her death, he wrote, "Oh, if I could see her once more, were it but for five minutes, to let her know that I always loved her, through all that. She never did know it, never."

Jesus told us that within us would flow rivers of living water. There's a dry and thirsty land, a desert parched for love in the people around us.

We wonder if Timothy was there with Paul when he wrote about him to the Philippians. Did he overhear Paul's dictation to his scribe? What an encouragement that would have been to him! Paul was not a capricious flatterer, motivated by insecure solicitousness. He was able to be direct and honest with his companions about things they needed to change, but he was also open and free to express his feelings of love.

As I write this, the faces of all the love-starved people I have known march before my mind's eye. If only they had had a parent or a significant friend in the formative years to express warm, accepting, emotional, and physical love. The unblessed children of unexpressive parents are everywhere. Disturbed husbands and wives bear the marks of the absence of healing affection upon their faces and in the frustrations of unfulfillment. Why are we so inhibited in expressing our feelings? Some are afraid they will not be received; others have tried and been rebuffed or misused; others have not had a deep feeling of being loved; others are just too concerned about their own inverted need to be loved; others are blocked by self-centered shyness; and still others withhold their love until the other person meets their standards or judgments.

Here's a good way to focus this for each of us. Ask yourself the questions, "Who are the people in my life who need to know they are loved? What is it in me that holds back my feelings? Do I want to be different? Do I really believe that Christ in me can break through my reserve and speak and touch and heal with warm affection?" How we answer that could change our lives!

Lord, help me to put into words and action the way I feel about the people of my life. I pray that no one

with whom I come in contact today will have to wonder how I feel about them. Amen.

How To Decide What's Important

PEOPLE ARE THE NUMBER ONE PRIORITY.

*They all look after their own interests,
not those of Jesus Christ. But Timothy's
worth you know, how as a son with a
father he has served with me in the
gospel. I hope therefore to send him just
as soon as I see how it will go with me;
and I trust in the Lord that shortly I
myself shall come also* (Phil. 2:21–24,
RSV).

Have you ever noticed how we subtly shift the values of the
world around us into what we suppose is important to God? We
baptize position, power, and prestige with spiritualizing rationali-
zation and are sure God wills for us what we want to achieve.
Yet the frenzied scramble for these very things often clogs our
effectiveness for him.

Paul had some great things to say about Timothy which become a personal challenge to us. "He really cares about you.
Everyone else is concerned only about his own affairs, not about
the cause of Jesus Christ." Timothy had been to Philippi with
Paul on his first visit and had gone ahead for the second visit.
Now he was to be sent back again to give comfort. Timothy
means "good comfort," and he had lived out his name. He was
the only one left with Paul who was free enough of concern
about his own affairs to give himself to the cause of Christ,

spelled out in the Philippians' needs. Others were too busy, but Timothy knew that there was enough time in any day to do the things God wanted him to do.

Timothy had learned from Paul himself what it meant to care and give comfort. He had been a young man when Paul first visited Lystra where he lived with Eunice his mother and Lois his grandmother. Timothy watched Paul pour himself out for people in proclaiming the gospel and caring for individuals. He observed his blood caked body thrown out of the city after being flogged mercilessly. And Timothy was so moved by Paul's life and limitless compassion, he wanted to give his life to Christ also. In Paul he had found a purpose for his own life—a vision of what God could do with a life completely under his control and a plan for his world through Christ. When Paul returned to Lystra, Timothy was ready to give all he had to Christ.

Through the years that followed, Timothy discovered that he had a gift of comfort which enabled him to care. How very gratifying for him it must have been to have Paul affirm the very thing which distinguished his life. He had time for people and their needs.

Most of us are overly concerned about our own affairs. Our time fills up with a daily round of demands and responsibilities. How do we know what's important? For Timothy, it was the cause of Christ. This challenges us with a question: "Is what I am doing advancing the cause of Christ or have I asked Christ to bless my causes?" There were some great men around Paul at this time—Mark, Luke, Silas—surely they were busy for Christ. Yes, but perhaps too busy to hear the cry of human need.

Dietrich Bonhoeffer said, "We must be ready to allow ourselves to be interrupted by God. God will be constantly crossing our paths and cancelling our plans by sending us people with claims and petitions. We may pass them by, preoccupied with our more important tasks, as the priest passed by the man who had fallen among thieves, perhaps—reading the Bible. When we do that, we pass by the visible sign of the Cross raised (in) our path to show us that, not our way, but God's way must be done. It is a strange fact that Christians frequently consider their work so important and urgent that they will allow nothing to disturb them. They think they are doing God a service in this, but actually they are disdaining God's 'Crooked yet straight path.' They do not want a life that is crossed and balked. But it is part of the discipline of humility that we must not spare our hand where it can perform a service and that we do not assume that our schedule is our own to manage, but allow it to be arranged by God." [7]

I had this experience the other day. A man poured out his heart to me. He confessed a sin which had hung him up for some time. After we talked it through, we prayed. Then I looked him squarely in the eye and said, "My friend, God loves you and forgives you." Then he said, "You know, I knew that, but I needed to hear it and feel it from someone else." We all know how he felt.

Exactly! God made us that way. We need each other. His greatest gifts are usually held for us to be given through others because his purpose is that we depend on him and that we be interdependent with one another. Your name may not be Timothy, but what that name means, "good comfort," can be the purpose of your life today.

> Lord Jesus, I am busy as a result of conscious choices of what I think is important. Forgive me when my schedule precludes people in need of comfort. I want to live by your agenda. I yield this day and its schedule to you. I believe there is enough time to do the things you will for me to do. Amen.

Who Is Your Epaphroditus?

EXPRESS THE BUFFER OF GRACE TODAY.

I have thought it necessary to send to you Epaphroditus my brother and fel-

low worker and fellow soldier, and your
messenger and minister to my need, for
he has been longing for you all, and has
been distressed because you heard that
he was ill. Indeed he was ill, near to
death. But God had mercy on him, and
not only on him but on me also, lest I
should have sorrow upon sorrow. I am
the more eager to send him, therefore,
that you may rejoice at seeing him again,
and that I may be less anxious. So receive
him in the Lord with all joy; and honor
such men, for he nearly died for the
work of Christ, risking his life to com-
plete your service to me (Phil. 2:25–30,
RSV).

We would be surprised if someday we came into church and saw a wash basin and a towel on the communion table as worship symbols. Yet, the symbolism would be correct as well as alarming. We are meant to be servants, and these symbols remind us of what Jesus said about our calling.

When the disciples reached the Upper Room, someone was missing: the servant to wash their feet. It was customary for a servant to wash the dust off the feet of guests. The disciples were aghast when Jesus took up the basin and towel and served them. "But he is Master, Leader, first of all!" the disciples said in alarm. "Why is he serving us?"

No example could have been more penetrating. But Peter wanted nothing to do with this . . . that is, until he realized that this was a condition to communion at the Last Supper. How like Peter we all are!

The impact is inescapable. If we are to be Christians, we are to care for each other's needs. Often the needs are as basic as this, but more often they are more complex and hidden. Together then, once we have ministered to one another, we are to serve the world as healed, equipped people.

Epaphroditus was the Philippians' gift to Paul. He brought

gifts for his support, but he himself became a gift of comfort and strength. That took some courage to become a personal attendant of a man awaiting trial on a capital charge. He had come as an emissary from the Philippians to see what he could do to help Paul. And he assumed the risk by staying with Paul in spite of the danger. He even became ill from the Roman fever which had swept through the city, but had remained faithful to Christ and Paul.

Now Epaphroditus was homesick. He was a long way from home and was concerned for his people's welfare back in Philippi. Yet he was torn by duty and loyalty to Paul. Distress and heaviness filled his heart. What did God want of him?

How easily Paul could have said, "Listen, Epaphroditus, you got yourself into this thing with me willingly. What's the matter with your faith? Don't you believe enough to have courage to stick this thing out? Stop thinking about yourself and your loved ones back home. If you loved Christ, you'd stop worrying. He never promised a bed of roses!"

No, instead Paul graciously smoothed out the way before Epaphroditus and gave him a new mission which gladdened his spirits. He was asked to carry a letter to the Philippians. Paul knew there would probably be those who might call him a quitter and a coward. That's the reason he took the care in a large segment of the letter to explain the courage and faithfulness Epaphroditus had shown.

I believe there should be a buffer of grace between Christ's people which enables them to make allowances for each other's weaknesses and human needs. We are to hold people to their best, yes; but what's best sometimes may be a retreat which will later produce a greater advance.

Paul's attitude to Epaphroditus was consistent with Jesus' symbol of being a servant. Paul reproduced the same loving care he had received from his Lord so often.

Who's your Epaphroditus? He may be at home or at work, in the church or in the community. What will it mean to take up the towel and the wash basin for him? The dust is not on his feet but in his inner life. The grace you express will give him the chance of a new beginning.

Lord, help us to be the kind of people who don't always look for the wrong motives in people. Give us a wide open heart to people's frailties—like the kind you have for us. When we look at it that way, you have been like Paul was to Epaphroditus all through our lives. Amen.

Problems, The Presence And Power

WE WILL ALWAYS HAVE PROBLEMS BUT
WE CAN STOP BEING THE PROBLEM.

*And in conclusion, my brothers, may the
Lord give you much joy* (Phil. 3:1).
Finally, my brethren, rejoice in the Lord
(Phil. 3:1, RSV).

My children are my best critics. On Sunday noon at dinner my son Andrew remarked, "I enjoyed your sermons this morning." I caught the emphasis on the plural. "What do you mean sermons?" "Well, ya know, the one you prepared to preach and the other two you preached after the last two 'and in conclusions.'" We all laughed at dad's misguided effort to say it all on one Sunday morning. My wife, Mary Jane, has often said, just before I leave to go to a speaking engagement, "When you say 'and now in conclusion,' do just that."

Paul's transitional use of a Greek expression has been translated in today's Scripture verse to sound like a preacher's concluding remark. Actually, most English translations miss the intent of the original language and therefore leave out the possibility of feeling the real force of Paul's thought patterns. The Greek word *loipon* literally means "as for the rest" and not "in conclusion" or "finally." This is not a point of false finish in Paul's letter. It is transition to another subject.

93

And that's the thing which gripped me as I thought about this verse. Paul's mind turns to a new problem and immediately to an old but faithful help. In chapter 3 he will deal with the divisive influence of a group outside the church which harassed the peace and unity of the Philippians. In the same breath he seems to say, "As for the rest, I want to say, go on constantly rejoicing in the Lord." Or to express it another way, "Rejoice in this next problem I want to discuss."

Problems and rejoicing. We don't think of them together, do we? Paul's exhortation is repeated often: Rejoice in problems. He doesn't seem to mean, "Rejoice that you have problems," but "Rejoice when problems come along." What does this mean?

The key to unlock the meaning is in the two translations we have used today. Each one stresses half of a whole truth. We are to rejoice, and the Lord will give us joy. That's the meaning of rejoicing "in the Lord." By that Paul means relationship. When a problem hits, our duty is to rejoice; the Lord's gift is joy. Remember that joy is a fruit of the spirit—a gift which cannot be experienced apart from the Giver.

Another way to say this is: When you get whacked with a problem, open yourself to a deeper relationship to the Lord. Don't focus on the problem but on the Lord's presence and power.

I am convinced that rejoicing comes simply from the realization that the Lord is present and will find a way to use every problem for our growth, and his purposes. It's actually feeling that repetitious movement of his presence which stirs the joy of his indwelling Spirit. That's why joy is indomitable and independent of circumstantial evidence.

Most of us have an inadvertent gear which shifts into place when a problem hits. What's yours? Some get frantic; others remain stoic. Some run off in all directions searching for solutions. Others pretend there's no problem. Many of us pout, "All I ever get is problems." And others shout, "Somebody up there forgot me!"

I have often entertained the distorted thought that someday I would be free of problems. Not so. Problems are the evidence of the Spirit of God continuing his creative purposes. Wherever he is at work, another force, the power of evil, is also at work. Conflict between the two cause our greatest disturbance. In every problem our task is to become receptive to what the Lord is seeking to create in that situation and to rejoice that he's at work, and his joy flows out of the inner depths of our being. We know that our Lord will win! The cross . . . resurrection . . . Pentecost . . . his living presence here now. Rejoice! He is working out his amazing good will . . . let go . . . trust . . . new love for him begins to flow . . . now joy leaps within us . . . and now peace. Blessed peace. Rejoice!

"As for the rest." What is the rest for today? There will be problems, be sure of that, but there will also be the Lord's presence. Rejoice at that.

> Lord, I need Paul's ability to think of problems and your power at the same time. Sometimes it's not easy to rejoice or be joyful. I get bogged down with problems and the illusive hope that someday I can solve them all. But I begin this day with two inseparable thoughts: I will always have problems, that's life. But I will always have you, and that's LIFE! Amen.

The "If" Syndrome

THE OBSTACLE OBSESSION IS THE SICKNESS
OF "IFY" CHRISTIANS.

It doesn't bother me to repeat what I have written before, and it will help make you safe. Watch out for those who do evil things, those dogs, men who insist on cutting the body. For we, not they, are the ones who have received the true circumcision, for we worship God by

95

his Spirit, and rejoice in our life in Christ
Jesus (Phil. 3:1-3).

Tears were streaming down her face as she left church. The theme of the service had been unqualified love: God's for us and the need for us to love unqualifiedly the people around us. The illustrations in the sermon had been painfully personal and many of them had dealt with relationships with family and friends. God had given this woman a great gift: He had shown her the agonizing portrait of her life. She was rankled, horrified and then disturbed by the dolorous emotional condition she had created in her house.

Later when we talked in depth, she gave me a handle to understand her problems. She said, "I've been an 'ify' Christian. You know, I will love you 'if.' I will accept you 'if.' I will give myself 'if' . . ." Her whole life had been developed around this manipulative syndrome. It was her way of getting what she wanted. Together we searched in her background for reasons for this behavior. As I suspected, she had been loved that way and was repeating the process. But life had been particularly harsh since the teen years, and the pattern had been embittered. Now it was used as an escape from the responsibility to love and care.

The term "ify Christian" has lingered in my mind. Many of us suffer from this syndrome of concurrent symptoms. It's a combination of criticalness, withheld affirmation and acceptance, and a deliberate attempt to see obstacles and not opportunities. The cause is a "righteousness deficiency" in our experience of our faith.

In Christ, God has made us "right" with himself. He has forgiven our sins through the cross and loves us unswervingly. If we will not accept this and try to establish a righteousness of our own (that is, to seek to win God's love by our goodness or perfection), a righteousness deficiency develops and the "if" syndrome shows in our relationships. We commit the ultimate blasphemy: We play "God" with ourselves and others and then perpetrate the worst crime of relational living . . . we judge and criticize and receive people only as they meet our ever increasing standards of qualification.

This was the basic problem of the Judaizers who harassed Paul's ministry and unsettled the early Christian church. I remember a British theologian friend who was in a debate over the question of prevenient grace. His opponent maintained that God's love was expressed after we believe and fulfill the demands of righteousness. My friend's response was undeniably direct, "You're a bloomin' Judaizer, that's what!" Few people in the room knew what he meant.

The Judaizers believed that Jesus was the Savior of Israel only and taught that a person could come to Christ to be saved only through the doors of Judaism. They insisted that all of the legal, ritual, and religious qualifications and demands of the Jews be fulfilled impeccably before a person could grow in Christ. Paul's obvious anger as he speaks of them in today's verse was caused by the way they tried to undo his teaching and ministry. They followed him wherever he went, contradicting his message of justification by faith and the righteousness of God through Christ. And they remained behind after he left a city to confuse the fellowship of grace in the newborn Christians.

Paul called them dogs. Strange twist. The Gentiles were often called dogs by strict Jews. He takes the very disparaging term the Jewish teachers would have used for Gentiles and flings it back in their faces.

But he calls them something else. He speaks of them as the "concision." This is the only time the term is used in the New Testament. Again, a clever twist. Paul's scholarship is showing a bit. The term meant mutilations forbidden by Mosaic law, such as were done in pagan rituals in Old Testament times. He uses this term to play on the Greek word for circumcision. The Judaizers insisted that all Gentile converts to Christianity be circumcised as a sign of their entrance into the true Israel. Circumcision was a crucial ritual to the Jews, done on the eighth day of a male child's life. Paul felt that putting this obstacle before a Gentile Christian was "ify." The love of God was not qualified by this outward sign. But further, Paul asserted that the church was the true circumcision through faith in Christ.

97

The Judaizers had mutilated the message of the gospel of God's righteousness and grace. They denied the freedom of forgiveness and demanded that the new Christians put God in their debt by the good works they had accomplished.

The Judaizing spirit is infectious. We all suffer from it at times. Whenever we place rules and regulations, rites and rituals, performance and perfection, standards and dogmas, as qualifications of either God's love or ours, we perpetrate the sickness. We become like the Judaizers when we put up external standards for ourselves before we will dare to let our spirits soar in grateful response to God's love. We wait for some magic time when we will have fulfilled our own expectations and believe we are worthy of God's acceptance. The time never comes! This cycle of condemnation robs us of the joy of being alive in the unearnable resources God makes available to us.

We also become Judaizers with the people in our lives. We withhold love, approval, and affirmation until some mysterious moment when people are worthy. This cranky negativism exudes a spirit of anxious insecurity in people, prompting them to feel they must do something to please us.

A church can develop a Judaizing spirit. Beliefs, practices, theological dogmas, denominational loyalties, cultural customs, local church loyalties, "sacred cows," are all put as obstacles which a man must fulfill before he's acceptable. Often it's difficult to get beyond these things to Christ. Paul gives us the triumphant alternative: "We worship God by his Spirit and rejoice in our life in Christ Jesus."

The other day, I had an encounter with a contemporary Judaizer. He had come to tell me about his new experience of speaking in tongues. I affirm this gift as one of the gifts of the Holy Spirit, so it was not difficult for me to respond and share his enthusiasm. Then the mood shifted. "Why don't you preach 'tongues'? You need to tell our people that tongues is the only undeniable sign that they have received the Holy Spirit."

As I pressed the point, I discovered that for this man speaking in tongues was a qualification for, and not a quality or result of, the gift of the Holy Spirit. Having witnessed the problems with people in whom tongues were induced forcefully and knowing the emotional sickness which can be expressed through a false use of this gift, I felt some of Paul's indignation over the Judaizers.

Who in your life needs to know that you are for them unqualifiedly? Think of them right now. What obstacles have you placed in their way of getting close to you or to the Lord? What are the "ifs," however pious and laudable they may be, that you are holding out for in the relationship?

Most of the things we want for people can come only as the result of the metamorphosis caused by God's forgiving grace. When we make results qualifications, there will be little result of our influence on people.

If you're a "bloomin' Judaizer," an "ify" person, you've got lots of company. We can all make a new start today with a fresh experience of God's unqualified love. That's the only hope of healing the syndrome. I'm willing, how about you?

> Lord Jesus, down through the years men have displayed a fantastic ability to confuse others about you. We are not very different today. I find the Judaizing, "ify" spirit in me often. I put up standards for people to measure up to before I give myself to them. How thankful I am that you don't treat me that way. I ask now for one gift for today: to begin to change my "ify" moods and stop Judaizing people. Thank you, Lord. I know that you have initiated this prayer and want to answer it even more than I wanted to pray it. Amen.

The Guilted Cage

WE SHAPE OUR CUSTOMS AND THEN OUR
CUSTOMS SHAPE US.

We do not put any trust in external ceremonies. I could, of course, put my trust

*in such things. If anyone thinks he can
be safe in external ceremonies, I have
even more reason to feel that way. I was
circumcised when I was a week old. I am
an Israelite by birth, of the tribe Benja-
min, a pure-blooded Hebrew. So far as
keeping the Jewish Law is concerned, I
am a Pharisee, and I was so zealous that
I persecuted the church. So far as a man
can be righteous by obeying the com-
mands of the Law, I was without fault.
But all those things that I might count as
profit I now reckon as loss, for Christ's
sake* (Phil. 3:3–7).

"He's a presbyterian Presbyterian, like us." The woman spoke
with an air of confidence and smug security. She had been raised
in one of the oldest churches in America, steeped in tradition.
The order of worship had been the same for eighty-seven years.
The ethos of the parish life gave the comfortable feeling of practices and customs which had been dutifully repeated for years.
Changes in anything from the order of worship or the color of
the choir robes were unthinkable.

The thing which caught my attention was that this woman
spoke about the services and activities of her church as if they
were pleasing to God. She really believed that God had ordained
their parish life and that any alterations would be blasphemous
to him. All that was done was an act of obedience to God as if
he could listen only to prayers which were prayed in the King
James English and with the same words as those used by John
Knox and John Calvin. There was nothing wrong with the customs; what was wrong was the sense of authority given to tradition as a divinely ordained way to please and placate God.

Could we say with Paul, "We do not put any trust in external
ceremonies"? That would be difficult for many of us. We all
develop cherished ways of doing things in our personal or institutional life which become a security to us. We shape our
customs and then our customs shape us. We become slaves to
sameness.

The difficulty comes in where we put our trust. Paul lists out all of the external things which could have been a source of security to him. Heritage. Ceremonial perfection. Ritual impeccability. Obedience to the Law. None of those things could make him righteous before God.

The Apostle had been set free from the guilted cage. Prior to the Damascus Road experience he was driven by a sense of guilt. He had to please God, earn his approval, fulfill the letter of the Law. All because of the wrong reason. He did the things which made him a good Pharisee because of his image of what he thought he ought to be. Yet he was headed in the wrong direction, driven by the wrong motives, accomplishing the wrong goals. Then he met the living Christ. His life was reoriented and refocused. His inner sense of guilt was healed by the forgiving love of Christ, and he was set free to live responsibly. Looking back over his own experience, he could boldly proclaim, "Now the Lord is the Spirit, and where the Spirit of the Lord is, there is freedom" (2 Cor. 3:17, RSV).

Today's passage is a profound analysis of the difference between guilt and grace, frustration and freedom, manipulation and maturity. Paul seems to be answering the basic question, "Why do we do what we do?" He says, in substance, "It is not that in our own resources we are adequate—our ability comes from God who has qualified us to share a new kind of relationship. Trying to fulfill the letter of the Law leads to guilt, the death of the soul; the Spirit of God alone can give life to the soul."

Huxley said that a man's worst difficulties begin when he is able to do what he likes. Not so. Our real difficulty begins when what we come to like is motivated by a fatuous compulsion of a sense of guilt. A life motivated by guilt becomes a guilted cage. We become entangled in the tender trap of doing what seems good because we feel badly; we are driven to do the right things for the wrong reasons; we are immobilized in reaction and unfree to act; we are the victims of turbulent, inner thoughts and seldom feel inner peace. Our accomplishments never match our expectations. The people of our lives feel the pressure of our unfilled dreams and often feel that what we do for them or with them is the result of unsatisfied psychic demands. We are not free!

The liberating truth of today's Scripture is that we are set free from the necessity to live to please God. We already are pleasing to him. He declared that once and for all in the cross. Now what we do can be an expression of praise rather than a condition of his approval. What a difference!

Today, let's consider the things we do and why we do them. Tradition, custom, habit? These may be fine. But do we think God will love us more for them? How much do we do as a free expression of love because of what he's done for us?

> Lord Jesus Christ, today I want to live my life as an expression of your love rather than as an effort to earn or deserve your love. Like Paul, I have tried about everything to prove my worth. Nothing satisfies. I am weary of doing the right thing because of guilt and not grace. Thank you for the limitless power of your love which sets me free from a guilted cage to fly and soar to new heights of joyous praise today. Amen.

Christ Is All Or Not At All!

CHRIST IS MORE IMPORTANT THAN THE THINGS WE DO FOR HIM.

Not only those things; I reckon everything as complete loss for the sake of what is so much more valuable, the knowledge of Christ Jesus my Lord. For his sake I have thrown everything away;

I consider it all as mere garbage, so that
I might gain Christ, and be completely
united with him (Phil. 3:8–9).

It's late at night and very quiet. The day has been full of speaking, counseling with people, and meeting with committees. Now I have a few moments for meditation, reflection, and honest reevaluation. I started the day with reading this verse from Philippians. It has been on the edge of my consciousness all day. At times it has haunted me and challenged my priorities.

The question has persisted all day. Now I can avoid it no longer. Can I say what Paul has said? Can I "reckon as loss" the things which mean so much to me? Could I throw everything away, consider it as garbage, so that I might gain Christ and be completely united with him? Just how important is the knowledge of Jesus Christ my Lord to me?

As I write this, I realize how much I need to experience the reality of this verse myself. I love my work, my church, my people, very much. I have had more than my share of public, professional, and personal affirmation. Education and background mean a great deal to me. Tonight my life unfolds before me. A sense of uncontrollable praise fills my heart. I know that I could not think a thought, write or speak a word, organize anything or lead anyone without my Lord's power.

Is anything I am doing for him more important than him? Nothing belongs to me! It's all his gift. But would I give it all up for him? Is the Lord more crucial to me than what I do in my ministry for him?

History is punctuated by instances of people who have become more committed to buildings, programs, and careers than Jesus himself. Our ministries can become so much an extension of our egos that we can lose the One for whom our ministries exist. Unless we allow Christ to minister to us we will use our ministry to minister to us!

The night noises sing persistently. The cool air sweeps through my study. I am alone for a few brief moments in a life otherwise filled with people and conversations. But now I realize that I am

103

not alone and that there is but one last conversation before I sleep. The One who never sleeps is here. My conversation in prayer with him is what makes all other involvements real. The question he asked Simon Peter beside the sea is the question he asks me right now. "Lloyd, do you love me more than anyone else? Do you love me more than your work for me, your phrases about me, and the praise you receive for your efforts for my cause?"

Suddenly the issues are painfully and poignantly clear. With Christ we have everything, without him, nothing we do, however spectacular, has meaning. Now I know again what I must rediscover every day: Christ must be all or he is nothing at all. Now I am ready to rest so that I may work tomorrow, not for the glory of the ministry but for him alone!

How do you feel about this verse? What does it do to you? Picture all the things you possess and have achieved. Put this book down for a moment. Now ask yourself, "Is any one of them more important to me than Christ as indicated by the way I spend my time, energy, or money?" If you are like me, the Lord has some disturbing things to say.

But this is an old problem. We're no different than Christians in any age. That may be true, but it does not have to be our cop-out. The creative process the Lord has put me through tonight must happen many times. Without this decisive encounter we could lose Christ in Christianity, churchmanship and ministries without meaning. Without Christ all that is garbage, isn't it?

Lord Jesus, we thank you for what you did in Paul to produce a verse like our text for today. In it you have given us the secret to power. Hear us now as we throw away, one by one, the things we clutch as false securities which make us ambivalent with you. Let us love in sincerity and practice. If we live like this, we shall know that we are children of the truth and can assure ourselves in the sight of God, even if our hearts feel guilty. For God is infinitely greater than our hearts, and he knows everything. Thank you, Lord, for setting us free from the power of rules and regulations and giving us the motivation to live responsibly in love. Amen.

How Changed Are My Ambitions?

WHAT IS THE DRIVING AMBITION OF YOUR LIFE?

All I want is to know Christ and feel the power of his resurrection; to share in his sufferings and become like him in his death, in the hope that I myself will be raised from death to life (Phil. 3:10, 11).

"You're a very ambitious young man! I only pray that you will be ambitious for something that's worth achieving." This penetrating observation was made by a seasoned old saint who could see the fires of ambition burning within me and was concerned that I may be heading for the right thing for the wrong reason.

I was the pastor of a new church. I wanted desperately to have the church grow and succeed. But my ambitions were ambivalent. I had the same burning desires for recognition, advancement, and popularity which burn within any 25-year-old, fresh out of graduate school. All of my goals were outwardly magnanimous. I wanted to build up the membership, construct a building of lasting beauty, and contribute to the work of the church in that area. But why? To what end?

I was challenged one day with the question: If you got to where you are going, where would you be? If you accomplished your goals, what would you have? If you attained your ambitions, what would you possess? I was shocked to realize that my ambitions were all mixed up. Primary, essential purposes were placed after what should be secondary goals. I wanted to build a great church, become an effective communicator, and be a creative pastor. Good ambitions, eh? I had decided that if I was to be a clergyman, I wanted to be the best I could. Laudable, indeed!

The same ambitious nature which had been charged up by the luscious taste of success in speech and dramatics now were baptized in the waters of religious activity. My inner nature was about to be invaded by my Lord and the long hard process of reformation of my character was about to begin.

About that time J. B. Phillips' translation of Philippians was off the press and into my hands for summer reading. I can still remember how shocked I was when the Holy Spirit used Dr. Phillips' translation of today's Scripture verse, Philippians 3:10: "How changed are my ambitions! Now I long to know Christ and the power shown by his resurrection: now I long to share his suffering, even to die as he died, so that I may perhaps attain, as he did, the resurrection from the dead."

I had to honestly ask, "What is my primary ambition?" I was deeply unsettled to realize that all my ambitions, however laudable, were self-generated and self-oriented. I made a covenant with the Lord that day to go through the prolonged and painful surgery of soul that would be necessary to experience as well as say that my only ambition was Christ himself.

What are the ambitions which drive you? Dryden was right: "Accurst ambition, How dearly I have bought you."

So many of the impelling ambitions of our lives, like mine as I began my ministry, are laudable and worthy of praise. In our culture, getting ahead, advancing professionally, gaining recognition, acquiring the comfort stuff of life, rising to heights of popularity, are all fine goals which fire our ambition. For many of us Christ is added as a side loyalty. Our time, energy, and money are spent on our true ambitions. We want Christ to help us get to our determined goals. He becomes a very necessary ingredient in success. We need him for strength, personal magnetism, guidance, and daily peace.

When we are driven by ambition, we will drive ourselves and the people around us. This is when we make dangerous compromises of our values. As De La Bruyère said, "The slave has but

106

one master, the ambitious man has as many masters as there are persons whose aid may contribute to the advancement of his future." The entangling alliances of life result. We use people to get to our ends.

Paul exposes a different ambition which reorders all others. He wanted to know Christ and experience the power of his resurrection. This then reordered everything else. He had been through all the false ambitions as a Hebrew Pharisee and then as a vigilant Christian worker. Now, in prison at the end of life he ended up where he wished he could have begun: with no other ambition than Christ himself.

I have spent a lot of time with people who knew they were about to die. A question I like to ask is, "If you could do it all over again, what would you do?" So many have said, "I would spend more time with Christ. I would give less of myself to things which distracted me from Christ. I would make Christ the passion of my life."

There are two parts of Paul's clarified ambition: to know Christ and experience the resurrection. To know Christ implies interpersonal relationship, not comprehension of facts. This is expressed in actual experience of his resurrection. The cycle of death and resurrection is interwoven into all of life. In every situation, with every person, in every decision or plan, there is the moment of death. Once we let go of our grip on life, the gift of God can be given. Our Lord wants to give us his direction, insight, and power. But not until we die to our own plan.

To share in Christ's sufferings means that we become involved with people to care for them even at the cost of our own convenience or comfort. But Christ, not helping the people, is our ambition. Once he is central, then, inadvertently, we relive his death and know his resurrection, and what we do with people is less manipulating and more liberating.

What about you? What are your ambitions? Really!

Lord, I confess that I have baptized my selfish ambitions in religious activity. I often want to have you as one of my ambitions while I press on with my own self-centered ambitions. Thank you for the creative

107

verve in me that longs to press ahead, develop, advance to new heights. I only ask that you will be the central focus of my ambition and nothing or no one else will replace that ultimate loyalty. Amen.

Well, Nobody's Perfect!

THE CLOSER TO CHRIST WE COME THE MORE WE FEEL LIKE WE HAVE HARDLY BEGUN TO KNOW HIM.

I do not claim that I have already succeeded in this, or have already become perfect (Phil. 3:12).

It's amazing! But I know it to be true from years of close observation of growing Christians. The point is this: The closer a person comes to Jesus Christ and a realization of his love and power, the more he feels he has to grow. The more a person learns, the more he discovers he does not know. When we think we have arrived spiritually, chances are that we have only reached an impasse of nondevelopment.

Paul comes down from the soaring heights of rhetoric in yesterday's assertion about experiential knowledge of Christ and the experience of the power of his resurrection. He has stated his purpose to know Christ better all the time, to have resurrection power surging through him, to be a joint-participant in Christ's suffering. The desire to be like Christ came from the Greek words, "Made conformable," which literally mean "to bring to the same form with another person." Now in verse twelve, he wants to honestly admit that he has not completely succeeded in attaining this or approaching it in all of life.

Paul then uses a verse which should help the perfectionists, "Or have already become perfect." The word "perfect" does not mean flawless or impeccable. It comes from an old verb, *teleios*, from the root *telos*, meaning end or purpose. Paul's end purpose was Christlikeness in every nerve and facet of his nature. He was not concerned about perfectionism, but purposefulness.

How often we get hung up on a petulant perfectionism over the details of living which has little to do with Christ's purpose for us. Most perfectionism is initiated in a desire to be good and adequate enough to earn God's love. Paul knew he had that so he could get on with the real business of being "in Christ"—to keep on working toward his purpose in experiencing Christ and his resurrection power.

Paul knew that he was not spiritually mature. There was so much more to discover, learn, and experience. How very challenging! Here is the most spectacular Christian who ever lived confessing his need to continue to grow in maturity. This is a true test of greatness: the acknowledgement of the need to keep on growing.

No one would ever say that he has learned all that was to be learned or that he now was spiritually mature. But I wonder, at times, about our passive resistance to growth. I meet few people who are voraciously hungry for more knowledge and experience of Christ. Our habits and time expenditure betray how much we believe that we need to grow. What are we involved in right now which is an expression of our hunger and thirst for more of Christ?

Satisfaction is a sure sign of an impasse of immobility. The evidence of the Spirit's work in us is an urgent dissatisfaction with our present level of growth. But how do I know where I need to grow in Christ?

Get with a Christian friend or loved one and dare to talk through the question: "How have I grown and where do I need to grow?" Review yesterday's verses ten and eleven as a basis of evaluation. How are you doing there? Then pray that Christ will show you where he wants you to grow.

> Lord Jesus, the closer I come in knowing you, the more conscious I am of the distance I have to come. The more I discover, the more I realize I don't know. The more I love you, the more I realize there is to

love. Thank you for loving me enough to withdraw the security of self-satisfaction and replace it with an urgency of getting on with the next stages to glory. Amen.

Running A Race We've Won Already

CHRIST'S GIFT IS THE FREEDOM TO FORGET.

Of course, brothers, I really do not think that I have already reached it; my one purpose in life, however, is to forget what is behind me and do my best to reach what is ahead. So I run straight toward the goal in order to win the prize, which is God's call through Christ Jesus to the life above (Phil. 3:13–14).

I asked an Olympic runner the secret of his success. His answer had profound implications for the Christian life and gave me the key to unlock the meaning of what Paul meant in this verse. This is what the runner said, "The only way to win a race is to forget all previous victories which would give you false pride and all former failures which would give you false fears. Each race is a new beginning. Pressing on to the finish tape is all that's important!"

This young man knew what he was talking about. He was right about athletic running and spiritual living.

The freedom to forget is a gift of the Master. He frees us to forget past achievements and failures so that we can press ahead to the goal. To remember is a magnificent capacity of our nature. Without it, we would be incapable of learning from past studies, experiences, and observation. With it we can build on the past and redeem the future.

Our minds are like computers. The other day I had the opportunity to hear and observe a computer organ. The sounds of a pipe organ are simulated in a very effective way. In addition to the basic organ, the computer is able to be programmed with the sounds of various ranks of pipes by the insertion of memory cards. Trumpets, special flutes, and other stops can all be added to the organ's basic sound by these cards which are inserted into a thin slot. The more cards inserted the greater the organ. But the thing which amazed me was the way the computer could be cleared and the memory factors removed with a flick of a switch.

As I watched this process, I thought about how wonderful it would be for human beings if we could heal memories as easily as the computer was cleared. Not so! We are all a composite of what we have done or what's been done to us. Our computer in the brain has tissue connections for all the memories, good and bad, of our lifetime.

The miracle of conversion is the transformation of our memories. When we open our minds to the healing of our memories, Christ is able to remove the hurt and sting and put our good memories into perspective, free of debilitating pride. We can literally forget what lies behind.

Recently, I was a part of a conference in which we tried to help people get in touch with their memories. I was amazed at how many excruciatingly painful, poignant memories we all carried just beneath the conscious level. We reached back into childhood and the families out of which we all had come. We drew our family table of childhood years and colored in each member of the family with appropriate colors. This dredged up unhealed memories of the personality constellations of childhood. We moved through the growing years and into teenage memories. Otherwise secure and competent people were helped to see and feel the influence of the past on present personalities and performance. Then we dealt with events in the past we wished we could relive and change. One by one, the memories were excavated and exposed to the healing love of Christ. Through tears and laughter, I saw people liberated to live much more abundant lives, free of the hidden hurts of the past. The surgery left only scar tissue. The malignancy and pain were gone.

Then we moved on to answer the question, "What achievements of the past keep you from daring new challenges for Christ?" We found that our security was often rooted in what we had done rather than what our Lord would do in us in the future. Some of the people actually were immobilized by a fear of failing to live up to the past. One man said, "If I could just live on my record like a champion who retires after winning, it would be a great comfort."

All of this gave me insight into what Paul was talking about in the race of the Christian life. He longed to forget both the grotesque things he had loved before he was a Christian and some of the inept things he had done as a Christian. Did his mind ever drift back to the persecution of the early church when he was a Pharisee? Of course! There were times he knew the same burning anxiety of reflection we all know. And after his conversion, he failed his Lord often. His confession of failure is found in his letters to the churches.

But with equal intensity, Paul wanted to forget the accomplishments of his life both before and after Christ grasped his life. On a human level, he had good reason for pride. No Hebrew could outshine him; few Christians equaled his commitment and accomplishments. Paul's focus was on what Christ would do with the future. The Greek text suggests that he "completely forgot" the past.

The goal for Paul's race was Christ. Christ was the finish tape for him. The verse means that he stretched forward, ran "flat out," toward the goal. This imagery is illuminating. Just as a winning runner forgets the opponents around or behind him and looks only at the goal, Paul forgot the past and focused on the next steps toward the goal. Remember that Paul was in prison when he wrote this. He had an indomitable trust in the Lordship of Christ over past and future time. He longed to become more like Christ in every thought and action.

The race of the Christian life is the only race that is run knowing we have won already. We belong to Christ and the life in him can only be more exciting as we press on. That gives us the vitality of a second wind.

There is nothing more disappointing than a runner who drops out of a race or a Christian who slacks up because he thinks he has reached the finish line. We always have a future and press on. Our attention is neither on the crowd in the grandstand or the other runners on the track but on the finish line. The more we concentrate on Christ and live with attention riveted on him, the more, inadvertently, we become like him in thought, value, attitude, and character. "As for us, we have this large crowd of witnesses around us. Let us rid ourselves of everything that gets in the way, and the sin which holds on to us so tightly, and run with determination the race that lies before us. Let us keep our eyes fixed on Jesus, on whom our faith depends from beginning to end. He did not give up because of the cross! On the contrary, because of the joy that was waiting for him, he thought nothing of the disgrace of dying on the cross, and is now seated at the right side of God's throne" (Hebrews 12:1, 2).

> Lord Jesus, we confess our memories to you. The good that gives false security and the bad which creates guilt. We want to be free from the past to run the race unencumbered by what has been. As we lift them up, one by one, we ask for your healing power to exorcise and liberate us. Then give us a second wind for the race toward the goal of a life completely immersed in your Spirit and transformed into your likeness. Amen.

The New Person Is You!

WE LEARN ONLY WHAT WE PUT INTO PRACTICE.

All of us who are spiritually mature should have this same attitude. If, however, some of you have a different attitude, God will make this clear to you. However that may be, let us go forward

according to the same rules we have fol-
lowed until now (Phil. 3:15, 16).

"My three sons seem to be wondering about the strange new man sleeping with their mother." This was the impelling statement which ended a letter from a man whom I had met at a conference for Christian leaders. The new man he was talking about was himself. At the conference he had made some disturbing discoveries about himself which challenged him to begin growing again. He needed to grow in his capacity of honest, open freedom with his family. But "holding true to what he had attained" meant putting into action the discoveries he made while at the conference. He would have lost the power he found if he had not done what he described in a letter.

He wrote, "You really put me on the spot when you pressed me to agree to write and let you know about the relational events with my family after my return home from the conference. But, your caring enough to ask made a tremendous impact upon me in a most needful way.

"In the past fifteen years of marriage, I can never before remember wanting to get home to my family—specifically, my wife. Last week, for the first time, it became something that I just had to do. I was truly in a hurry to see them all. When I arrived, my oldest son was getting ready for a date. I knew that talking then would probably cause him to be late, but it was Saturday night and with Sunday to be another jam-packed day, I knew I couldn't wait until Monday. I sat with my family and poured my heart out to all of them—and to each of them. It didn't 'feel' good at all, but, then, neither does any other kind of surgery. For me, it was simply a confession of my need for each of them, and they responded to it beautifully! Before I finished, I affirmed each of them individually, but in front of the others. To say that it was a great experience is an understatement. To say that 'everything is all right now' is a lie. But, healing has begun, as you and I both knew it would, so much so, in fact, that my three sons seem to be wondering about the strange new man sleeping with their mother."

The sickening sameness of this man's life had been exposed, and he was on the way to new growth.

This is what Paul wanted for his dear friends in Philippi. Epaphroditus had brought him word that some of the Philippian Christians had fallen into the false idea of "sinless perfection." They reasoned that they were perfect in Christ—their sins had been forgiven, and they were liberated from the necessity to change. This is the true meaning of the verse, "If, however, some of you have a different attitude, God will make this clear to you."

There is a releasing idea here. God is the enabler of the urge to change and be different. When we force people to change, the result is that they spend so much energy reacting to us that there is little change. If we spent as much time in prayer for people about their need to change as we do trying to change them, what a difference it could make.

My friend at the conference had been changed by caring and deep concern. Perhaps our problems today are but the exposure of the next area of our need to change.

What would your image, family, and friendships be like if a new person were to come home, and that new person was you?

> Lord Jesus, growing in any area of life is never easy. I confess my need to grow, my desire to grow, my commitment to grow. Now in the silence of this time of prayer, show me what I must do to hold true to what you showed me are the areas for growth as a person today. Amen.

The Imitation Of You

WHAT IF EVERYONE IN THE WHOLE WORLD WERE LIKE YOU IN PERSONALITY AND ATTITUDE?

Keep on imitating me, brothers, all of you. We have set the right example for you; so pay attention to those who follow it (Phil. 3:17).

How would you like to reproduce what has happened to your faith in the lives of others? Do you have the feeling that you would like everyone to discover what you have found? Can you say to the world around you, "Hey world, this is living! Man, this is life as it was meant to be lived!"

Unless we believe that what's happened to us in our relationship with Christ ought to happen to everyone, then probably too little has happened to us. If we don't believe in what's happened to us, nobody else will.

But Paul goes even deeper than that. With alarming audacity, he says, "Keep on imitating me." That to me is the great test of the dynamic of our Christian experience. If we are not so excited about what we have found that we want everyone to experience it, then we have not found very much.

When Paul appeared before King Agrippa (in Acts 26:24–30), he proclaimed the winsome power of his life in Christ. Agrippa responded, knowing full well that Paul was seeking to have him find the faith he had experienced, "In this short time you think you will make me a Christian?" Notice Paul's bold response, "Whether a short time or a long time, my prayer to God is that you and all the rest of you who are listening to me today might become what I am . . ." There it is again, the same confidence: imitate me! As I write this, I wonder if I can say that—at home, at work, with my friends? What about you? If not, why not?

I know, you're probably ahead of me with the question which grips the jugular vein of the Christian witness: "How can I, with all my imperfections, set myself up as an example? Why would you want anyone to imitate me with all my hang-ups and inadequacies?"

That's to misunderstand Paul. He was very honest with the

116

Philippians about his goofs and failures. What he wanted them to imitate was his experience of God's grace and forgiveness. How he handled his failures was an invaluable part of his witness to Christ in his life. He did not want people to know how great he was, but how great God had been in his life.

Many Christians never get on with sharing their faith because of all that they know is wrong in their own lives. "I am not worthy," we say. Of course we're not. If we ever thought we were, we would be completely unusable to our Lord. What he longs to expose to the world and have others imitate in us is our dependence on him and the joy and love his Spirit can produce in us.

After Jesus had washed the disciples' feet, he said, "I have given you an example, that you also should do as I have done to you." The early church was reminded of the same basic calling of all Christians: "For to this you have been called, because Christ also suffered for you, leaving you an example, that you should follow in his steps" (1 Peter 2:21, RSV). We are to allow Christ to re-produce his life uniquely in each of us. His love, character, and passion for people's need is to be reproduced in us. When it is, we become an example to others.

How about an experiment today? Let's live through the day with an acute sensitivity to our actions and reactions, our feelings, and our handling of difficulties. Would we want others to live like that? Can we say to the people in our lives, "Keep on imitating me"?

Lord, guide me as I seek to share my humanity with others and communicate what you are doing with a person like me. It's a bit frightening to think of being an example of the Christian life for someone else or of having someone imitate me because of you. Yet Lord, I know that I am reproducing myself and my attitudes in the people around me all the time. Help me to discover the kind of vision of life in Christ which people will see today, not in my perfection but in what you can do with my imperfection. Amen.

A Trip Without Baggage

WHEN YOU'RE TRAVELING WITH THE LORD,
THERE IS SOME OF THE BAGGAGE YOU DON'T
NEED.

*I have told you this many times before,
and now I repeat it, with tears: there are
many whose lives make them enemies of
Christ's death on the cross. They are
going to end up in hell, for their god is
their bodily desires, they are proud of
what they should be ashamed of, and
they think only of things that belong to
this world* (Phil. 3:18, 19).

When I was a student and sailed across the Atlantic to Scotland
to do advanced studies in theology, I remember a sticker which
was placed on some of our luggage. All the pieces which we
would not need during the trip were prominently marked, "Not
needed during voyage."

I remember leaning over the railing to watch the stevedores
load all the baggage marked with that sticker into the hold of
the ship. It took a long time to load those pieces of luggage and
trunks. Then I observed the people who had come aboard and
overheard their conversations as they walked the decks. As I
looked into their faces, I realized that many people were still
carrying their baggage—but of a very different kind—deep inside them. The baggage of bad memories—personality traits,
patterns of thought, prejudices, fears, and reservations—seemed
to load many of them down heavily. I recall how I wished I
could have taken some of those things inside of me and some
inside of others and gathered them all together under the desig-
nation, "Not needed for the voyage."

Paul was concerned about some of the Philippians who had come into the Christian life with heavy baggage of philosophical convictions which were inconsistent with the gospel. In earlier passages he had dealt with the Judaizers. Now he levels his concern on a philosophic school of thought which was prevalent in the Philippian church. There were some of the Greek Christians who had been Epicureans and had taught that satisfaction of the physical appetites was the highest purpose of man. Many of them carried this belief into the Christian life and twisted the basic understanding of grace. The baggage of self-indulgence had distorted the voyage. It led to a heresy called antinomianism, lawlessness. In substance these people said, "God's grace is freely given, he loves and forgives us, so do what pleases and satisfies."

They did not fool Paul. He knew his Greek classics. In this passage from Philippians, he was probably thinking of the Epicurean idea of the god of the belly. Cyclops in Euripides said, "My flocks which I sacrifice to no one but myself, and not to the gods, and to this my belly, the greatest of gods: for to eat and drink each day, and to give one's self no trouble, this is the god of wise men." The effort to live a life free from responsibility and involvement actually became the heaviest baggage of all.

That kind of fuzzy thinking and irresponsible Christianity is still around. I talked to a young man the other day whose quest for the "feeling" of the faith had completely blocked out any kind of caring about other people. He had missed the truth that Christ has set us free to care about people and his world. There is this new wave of antinomianism—that is, anti-responsibility, anti-regulation—Christianity infiltrating the churches today. The emphasis is on a feeling of the Lord, an assurance of his love through esoteric experiences of his presence, and a high emotionalism which negates thinking and follow-through for people in need.

If Paul were writing to our day, he would probably expose this diminutive god of feelings. He would want to check the baggage of dependence on any previous experiences of our Lord which we would demand to have repeated in order to have as-

119

surance and security in our faith. Whatever gifts of the Spirit we might have received or special visions we might have encountered, he would still want to know what was happening to the lives of people around us through our love and concern.

But there is another kind of contemporary Epicurean in the churches today. He is the person whose own physical and personal needs always come before our Lord and faithfulness to him. Our body comforts—how and where we live, what we eat and how much, how we feel and what we spend to feel all right —all are contemporary Epicurean gods many of us worship and pay homage to with millions of dollars every week. How we look, what we wear, the luxuries we taste . . . ah . . . how "good" is the good life?

If someone had only our bank check stubs to use in writing our biography, what would he write? What values, convictions, and beliefs would he discern from what we spend and save?

Or try this on for size. If our bodies were our only autobiography, what would the world around us read about what we hold to be crucial and sacred?

Paul's cutting caution is that we can become enemies of the cross. Jesus said that people were either for him or against him. Paul says here that we can actually become an enemy of the cause we say is our life. We can live lives that are such a contradiction to what we say we believe that we end up on the enemy side.

When Peter wanted to dissuade Jesus from the implications of obedience to God and the eventuality of the cross, Jesus said, "Get behind me, Satan." Peter had become a tool in Satan's hand. He was working against the purposes of his Master. He was on Satan's side!

The Philippians Paul was concerned about were those who had watered down the gospel, distorted Christian freedom, and taken the cross out of the gospel. Watch out for any teaching or preaching which leaves the cross obscure or distorted. It's a sure test of an authentic proclamation that it leads us to the cross and then to costly caring about others.

What are the beliefs which are inconsistent with the gospel, the experiences which don't lead to obedience, the patterns of living which deify our bodily wants? They need to be marked, "Not needed for the voyage!"

Lord Jesus, the Scripture for today is downright disturbing! Am I among the enemies of the cross by the way I live? What beliefs and prejudices have I carried as impediments? Forgive any aspect of my life or attitudes which keeps me from walking humbly with you, open to the truth about myself, regardless of how much it hurts. I know that it is possible to be your follower and yet live a contradiction. Lord, help me to be honest about that with you today. Amen.

A Colony Of Heaven

HEAVEN BEGINS IN THE CHURCH, AND THE
CHURCH IS TO BRING HEAVEN TO SOCIETY.

*We, however, are citizens of heaven, and
we eagerly wait for our Savior to come
from heaven, the Lord Jesus Christ* (Phil.
3:20).

Malcolm Muggeridge, the well-known British columnist, world famous for his caustic wit as editor of *Punch,* has written a searching spiritual autobiography entitled *Jesus Rediscovered.* He exposes the realization during the past ten years of his life that despite all the shortcomings of organized religion Jesus Christ and the Gospels do have a meaning. He expresses a penetrating truth which sets in ridiculous perspective our longing for security in what we have and can achieve. This is what he rediscovered: "This sense of being a stranger, which first came to me at the very beginning of my life, I have never quite lost, however engulfed I might be at particular times . . . and circumstances, in earthly pursuits—whether through cupidity, vanity,

121

or sensuality, three chains that bind us, three goads that drive us, three iron gates that isolate us in the tiny dark dungeon of our ego. For me there has always been—and I count it the greatest of all blessings—a window never finally blacked out, a light never finally blacked out. The only ultimate disaster that can befall us, I have come to realize, is to feel ourselves to be at home here on earth. As long as we are aliens, we cannot forget our true homeland, which is that other Kingdom Christ proclaimed." [8]

Muggeridge expresses the essence of Paul's descriptive imagery of Christians as "citizens of heaven." The words Paul used could be translated "commonwealth of heaven" or "colony of heaven." The Philippians could easily catch the implied meaning. As Roman citizens, they were a colony of Rome in Macedonia. Their customs, laws, dress, and loyalties were all those of Roman citizens. They lived as Romans in an occupied foreign land.

This is what the church is meant to be in the world. We live together as a colony of heaven in an occupied territory. Our ultimate loyalty, customs, values, and quality of life are not of our culture but of our Lord and his Kingdom. The church is to be a foretaste of eternal life, an experience of heaven in miniature.

Our worship is to be a celebration of the resurrection. All of life is an Eastertide. We are alive forever and our hymns, prayers, and proclamations are to remind us of our true citizenship and help us reaffirm that heaven is our true home. Christ, not a contemporary, human leader, is to be our ultimate guide. Our allegiance is to the Kingdom of God, and the nation in which we live is to have secondary loyalty. The mode of our life is to be patterned after the gospel and not our culture. When we are together in the fellowship, we are to reaffirm our eternal citizenship and reclaim our eternal life. Our pledge of allegiance is "Jesus Christ is Lord" and "Those who believe in him shall not die but have eternal life." Life in the church is meant to be an earthly expression of the heavenly realm.

What this means for us is dependent on what we think heaven is like. I have always considered it in terms of relationships. We will be in relationship with our Lord, free of all our human limitations. We will know him as he is and will be known as we will be in complete reconciliation, harmony, and limitless love. We will know and love each other free from human fear, competition, and anxiety. We will be completely one with our Lord and with each other. As Paul put it in 1 Corinthians 13:12, "For now we see in a mirror dimly, but then face to face. Now I know in part; then I shall understand fully, even as I have been fully understood" (RSV).

Today's Scripture passage from Philippians echoes this same hope. Our weak, mortal humanity will be changed in our own personal resurrection. The same power which raised Jesus will raise us to life with him forever.

This is difficult for many of us to grasp. Our loyalty is to this life and our most significant citizenship is to our nation. We almost feel disloyal to America to say we are citizens of heaven. I remember how difficult it was for me to register as an alien when I was a student in a foreign land. Childhood conditioning made me suspicious of all "aliens." But just as I was patriotically loyal to America while I was a temporary alien in Scotland, so too, in a spiritual sense, I am an alien in our culture with my citizenship in heaven.

Many of the greatest patriots of American history loved God more than their country or culture and therefore were most vigilant and persistent to bring the true justice of God into the formation and growth of our government. Often the most socially responsible Americans are those whose eternal citizenship is in heaven.

I remember the accusation of a social revolutionary who completely missed this truth when he said, "One world at a time. You Christians are so concerned about your future life, you forget to live now. You are so worried about eternity that you don't think enough about how you are living right now. If you were as involved in caring about this world as you are in preparing for the next, you would do something about conditions in society right now."

This man was deploring the Christian's preoccupation with heaven and eternal life while society suffered injustice and the dehumanization of people. He had settled for a half truth. The

Christians who live irresponsible lives while people suffer are those whose loyalties are mixed and have made false gods of the securities of this world. I have found that Christians who are confident of their eternal life are often most involved in the needs of people. Eternal security most often is an impelling motive for caring concern during the years of life here on earth. The lack of fear of death and dying has liberated them to become socially responsible people where they live and work. Some of the greatest social reform movements have been led and staffed by those who knew that heaven was their ultimate destination and lived with the security and assurance of eternal life. As long as we have to stuff the brief years of this life with feverish activity to find meaning, we will twist and distort our reason for being.

I have always been fascinated by the progression of Paul's thought in 1 Corinthians 15. His declaration of the transformation we shall know in our own resurrection to the full experience of our eternal citizenship is followed by ethical implications for our life now.

First he says, "For this perishable nature must put on the imperishable, and this mortal nature must put on immortality. When the perishable puts on the imperishable, and the mortal puts on immortality, then shall come to pass the saying that is written: Death is swallowed up in victory. . . . But thanks be to God, who gives us the victory through our Lord Jesus Christ" (15:53, 54, 57, RSV).

Then he spells out what we are to do now: "Therefore, my beloved brethren, be steadfast, immovable, always abounding in the work of the Lord, knowing that in the Lord, your labor is not in vain" (15:58, RSV).

The purpose of the church as the colony of heaven and Christians as citizens of heaven is to live together in an ever increasing experience of the reality of heaven. Then as responsible participants in time and space, we are to do everything we can to bring that reality into all of life in our culture and nation.

Is your church a colony of heaven? To what extent is the Kingdom of God changing the society in which your church exists? What are the practical steps our Lord lays upon you and me for both the life of our churches and their ministry in society?

> Lord, thank you for the sense of being a stranger amid the things which are supposed to bring happiness. Our hearts are restless to rest in you. We are displaced persons in the world until you make us replaced persons in our society to bring heaven's reality to everyday life. I want to be part of your penetrating change of the church to be a colony of heaven. And then, I want to give myself to bring a taste of heaven on earth. Lord, show me how and where! Amen.

I Don't Believe In Religion!

ENJOYMENT EVANGELISM HAS A WINSOME
CONTAGION WHICH IS UNDENIABLE.

So, then, my brothers—and how dear you are to me, and how I miss you! How happy you make me, and how proud I am of you! (Phil. 4:1).

The other day while I was waiting to give an address at a high school graduation, my mind drifted back to my teenage years. If a clergyman had spoken at my graduation, I would have turned him off before he ever reached the speaker's rostrum. My experience with religious people had been so negative, so life-denying, so up-tight, that the last person I would have listened to would have been a professional religionist. I found them dull, unrealistic, and a walking set of pious, glib phrases.

I had left the church and organized religion when I was 13. The day that I decided never to enter the door of a church

125

again is indelibly seared into my memory. It was in the middle of an exciting ball game that I heard my mother's voice calling across the field. I knew what she wanted. It was time for the Youth Fellowship group to meet at church.

I had to get changed and all dressed up and go to church. Once there, I was even more uncomfortable. The elders of the church got all the kids into the sanctuary and decided no one was going to leave until we all believed in God and "got religion." The leader said, "All those who believe in God stand up; those who don't, sit down." Now the possibility that there might be a God and that he wanted me to believe in him wouldn't have been so bad if it hadn't been for those religious people who exemplified what might happen if I believed. Everything about them seemed to deny life. They looked as if joy had gone out of style and that grimness was next to godliness. So I sat down. I will never forget the old elder who came up and down the aisles looking for those sitting down. He looked me in the eye and shook his finger at me and said in a rasping voice, "Young man, if you don't believe in God you are going to go where the buzzards are!" Well, that might be better than being any place near where he was! So I got up and left the church, slamming the door behind me. As I walked home, the old street lights were flickering in the dusk. The light cast an eerie shadow before me. "My God, the buzzards!" I cried, and ran all the way home. But when I reflected on what had happened to me, I thought, "How stupid! If that's religion, I've had enough." From that day on I resisted religiosity, "God talk," and churchy people.

It was in college that I met a group of people who were so alive, so dynamic, so joyous, that I wanted to find what they had found. I was amazed to discover that the reason they were so life-affirming was they believed in God. But they were not religious in the stuffy sense, if religion is man's effort to win, serve, and placate a power greater than himself. These people seemed to have a relationship with a God who had reached them, loved them, and had given them an exciting strategy for life. They cared about people, were deeply involved in student life, and had an affirmation of life which attracted me. Through

126

them I learned that God loved me just as I was. This filled the aching void in my insecure, inner self. They were not judgmental, but expressed a delight in me that helped me love myself.

After this experience of God's love, I changed my vocational plans from speech and dramatics to spending my life communicating to people the same love I had found. I became a clergyman, not to become religious, but to spend all of my time sharing a quality of joy and freedom which comes when you know you are deeply loved and forgiven. I have been at it ever since and am just as unreligious in a formal, negative sense as I was when I went to college.

Some time ago I sat down next to a student on an airplane. After I found out where he went to school, he asked me what I did for a living. I told him I was a communicator of life. That didn't satisfy. "No, I mean what kind of a job do you have?" he asked. Finally, I admitted that I was a clergyman. "Listen," he said, "don't give my any god talk. I don't believe in religion!" "Neither do I!" I responded. This amazed him. I told him that my business was people and introducing them to an abundant life. We were off! We talked incessantly all the way to Chicago. He wouldn't let the conversation lag for a moment, and when we landed, he followed me all the way into the terminal and to the cab stand. He wanted life, and so do we all. Since then we've exchanged letters, and I have seen him several times.

During that first visit, though, it came out that he was really hung up about what to do with his life. He had experimented in the dope scene in a desperate effort to dilate his consciousness to find meaning and purpose. And at that very moment he was in turmoil about his sex life with the girl to whom he was pinned. I asked him what he would do with his life if he knew he could have limitless power to love and care for people. "Well, man, if you put it that way, let me tell you . . ." He was on the way as he focused some exciting goals. Eventually, he asked God to guide his life and accepted God's love for him.

When our goal is to communicate life and not a religion, we can enjoy the people we are seeking to help. Enjoyment evangelism is contagious. When a person feels affirmed and enjoyed, he will take seriously our witness.

127

This again is shown as in Paul's expression of enjoyment of the Philippians. Having clarified that, he now could say some crucial things about how they were to stand firm in their new life.

I had a conversation with an old friend the other day. After all the surface catching up, our eyes met and we dared to ask the question which had rumbled beneath the surface—"How are you really? How's your life? What's happening to you as a person?"

If you and I had a personal time like that, the thing I would want to ask and have you ask me is, "What do you want out of life? What are your goals, your dreams, your wildest expectations for the future?"

One day a psychiatrist friend of mine in Princeton got one of those "strike it rich" sweepstakes letters from *Life* magazine: "You have been selected as the fortunate participant in a special offer which could make you the richest man in Princeton. Your name will soon be listed among the wealthy and prodigious people of Princeton. All you do is take a six-year subscription to *Life* and your name will be added to the drawing. You may win!"

My friend's answer is a gem of rhetoric. This is what he wrote: "In your letter you offer to make me the richest man in Princeton. I want you to know that I am the richest man in Princeton. In addition to this, I enjoy a quality of life so exciting, it makes *Life* magazine read like an old Mother Goose story. For all these good reasons, I am asking you to remove my name from that silly contest—a contest which cannot possibly do me any good because all it offers is money. Who needs it when he has *Life*—and I don't mean your magazine."

Life with a capital "L"—that's what it's all about.

> Lord of the way, the truth and the life, I thank you that what I can share with people is not more religion but life . . . as you lived it, as we can live it in you, and as you live it in us. Help me to be so alive today in the quality of your abundant life that I will be able to love and care and introduce people to you and your life-transforming power. Amen.

Keep Short Accounts!

*Euodia and Syntyche, please, I beg you,
try to agree as sisters in the Lord* (Phil.
4:2).

We sat and talked late into the night. The couple had shared with me the fact that they could not stay together any longer. They seemed to be at odds on every issue and concern of their lives. The complicating factor was that they deeply loved each other and wished they could get along. Both believed in Christ but could not find the power of their faith for this frustration.

"There's a great big wall between us, built by both of us," the man explained. "It's so high we can hardly see each other anymore," the wife added. Both expressed the wish that there could be some way to break the wall down and get together, but every time they started to take the stones of resentment out of the wall to look at them, the anger was set off all over again. "I guess we were never meant to be together," they concluded with resignation.

"I don't believe that!" I asserted. Then I went on to suggest that perhaps dismantling the wall was a second step. I suggested the possibility of their climbing the wall and living on each other's side for a period of time. "What would it be like if you were to experiment with defending each other from the other's side of the wall?" They didn't think it would work, but agreed upon a month's experiment before going to their lawyers. I asked them to take one-half hour each day during the experiment, each taking fifteen minutes of uninterrupted time to talk about their hopes and dreams for life and what frustrated them in realizing them. Neither was allowed to comment or criticize the other during this period.

I saw them again at the end of the experiment. They were both amazed at what they had found on the other side of the wall and what they had come to see in each other. Then they said, "Now we are ready to dismantle the wall."

That was not easy for either of them. But after the long, painful process had been completed, the problem they faced was maintaining the oneness they had achieved with God's help.

I shared with them a prescription for healthy emotional living which I have rediscovered and practiced for years. The only way to come together and stay together in a truly satisfying relationship is to keep what I call short accounts emotionally. They both wanted to make it work so they were eager to learn what I meant.

I explained that we all need emotional conversion as Christians. That means we accept Christ's love for our emotional nature. His love for us enables us to be honest with him and each other about our feelings. Most of us tend to hide how we feel. The result is that we pretend about what's inside us and simulate the emotion we think is expected. Repression causes depression. Sublimation results in compulsive patterns. Projection develops blaming others. Honesty about how we feel lets the steam out of our inner boiler. My friends had gotten into their trouble because they back-logged the ledger with unexpressed feelings.

Keeping short accounts heals emotional tension. The ledger should be cleared each day. The sun should not go down on unexpressed emotion. Our task is not to attack with accusations and admonitions, but simply to share with others how we felt in a certain situation. We all have a right to our feelings. Another person can deal with how what he did made us feel. That's okay. It liberates him to share how he felt. Then feelings can be dealt with, forgiven and healed.

When we harbor feelings, they build up and blow in an unrelated situation where our punishment of another person does not fit the crime. We have all experienced times when our emotional blast-off has been excessive and inadvertent because of the pressure within us.

Paul was deeply concerned about this in the relationship of two women in the Philippian church. After he said he would tell them how to stand firm in the Lord, his mind went first to

130

this conflict which had come to his attention. It was as if he were saying, "If you want to remain a strong, healthy Christian, deal with your conflicts quickly and decisively."

Think of how long these two women must have been at odds. The news of their separation had reached Paul in Rome. It took a long time for a messenger to travel to Rome from Philippi and an equally long time for this letter to be returned by Epaphroditus. We can only imagine how their feelings festered in this long hiatus. They had kept long accounts of grievances.

These women had not lived up to either their names or to their calling in Christ. Euodia actually means "prosperous or successful journey," and Syntyche means "pleasant acquaintance." Paul was urgently concerned that they become reconciled. There has been much expositional speculation as to what was the nature of their conflict. The fact that it was not clarified broadens the implication of Paul's admonition to be inclusive of the many things which we tabulate in our accounts against one another. He uses a very strong word in his admonition. "I beg you, please," means exhort, plead, urge. Everything he has written in the letter about unity is now specifically applied to these two leading women in the church. He longs for them to be of the same mind in the Lord. We are reminded of his challenge in chapter two: "I urge you, then, make me completely happy by having the same thoughts, sharing the same love, and being one in soul and mind." I believe this is what he meant when he challenged them to agree as sisters in the Lord. Because he put it in the context of their relationship with the Lord there was urgency not only for the peace and unity of the church, but his power was available to help them forgive and work out their hostilities.

The Ephesians needed to hear the same challenge: "And do not grieve the Holy Spirit of God, in whom you were sealed for the day of redemption. Let all bitterness and wrath and anger and clamor and slander be put away from you, with all malice, and be kind to one another, tenderhearted, forgiving one another, as God in Christ forgave you" (Eph. 4:30–32, RSV). Conflict among Christians is not unusual, then or now.

The application of these moving words becomes very practical. The problems between people will not go away through magnanimous overlooking of past hurts. Painful, specific encounter and confrontation in the presence of the Lord's motivating, enabling Spirit is the only healing.

What about us today? With whom do we need to clear the hostility ledger? Today's the day! Here are the four steps to healthy relationships:

1. To own my feelings.
2. To receive the Lord's forgiveness where the fault is mine.
3. To clear the feeling ledger with the person I have hurt or who has hurt me. (Not with someone else where gossip and not confession is so tempting.)
4. To dare to keep short accounts within each day and settle accounts before the sun goes down whenever humanly possible with face to face encounter or with the phone or letters when that is an impossibility.

> Lord Jesus, I want to keep short accounts with you and the people of my life. I realize that anytime I decide to internalize my feelings, I build steam in the emotional boiler inside. I have falsely thought that was Christian magnanimity. I now know it's cowardice and will eventually strain relationships. Give me the courage to clear the ledger each day. Amen.

The Wound Healers

TO BE "IN CHRIST" IS TO BE THE "INTERFACE" BETWEEN PEOPLE IN CONFLICT.

And you too, my faithful partner, I want you to help these women; for they have worked hard with me to spread the gos-

pel, together with Clement and all my
other partners, whose names are in God's
book of the living (Phil. 4:3).

I have a friend who sees his particular gift to be a wound healer. He's not a medical doctor or a psychiatrist, and he is not a professional clergyman. But he has a remarkable ministry. He is an engineer by avocation and a healer of relationships by vocation. Someone once asked him what he did for a living. His response was remarkable. "If by 'living' you mean what is my purpose for being alive, it is to be a wound healer. I earn my upkeep by being an engineer."

What he meant was that he has realized that his calling is to help people who are at odds to find new ways to accept each other and to communicate. He cannot stand by and watch people hurt and disturb each other because of misunderstanding and unresolved wounds. He feels that the interface between people in conflict is where he ought to be to help open forgiveness and new trust. This is not a compulsion with him but a genuine calling. He deliberately asks for the Holy Spirit's power to lay his life down in the breach between people and be a bridge over which they can go to find each other again. This man has studied and prayed to develop skills of reconciliation and renewal between people.

We all have a calling to be wound healers. This is what Paul is saying to the members of the Philippian church about the conflict between Euodia and Syntyche. He addresses a particular leader in the church, but his message is urgent for all. He uses some very strong language. Help these women! Lend a hand with them in settling those differences! The urgency is motivated by Paul's concern for the peace and unity of the church. When anyone is disturbed and separated from another, it is the concern of the whole fellowship. A virulent poison of discord can flow through the Body of Christ, the church, and cause a crippling ineffectiveness in the witness to the power of the gospel. The church is to be in its fellowship what it wants to communicate to the world.

Paul is saying that he wants the brothers and sisters in Christ of these women to act initiatively to heal the wounds. This was not a pleasant luxury but an absolute necessity. As a matter of fact, healing wounds was one of the essential ways of standing firm in Christ.

I remember two women in the first congregation I served as a student pastor. They had not spoken to each other in years. Each sat on a different side of the sanctuary in worship. Neither spoke to the other at meetings of the Women's Association. The hurts and hostilities were deep and angry. Other members of the church would smile in amused toleration of this condition which had festered as a thorn in the flesh of the congregation. I can remember the inconsistency I felt every time I preached about love and the power of Christ to heal differences. Most of the members had no expectation that things would ever be different.

I brought the conflict before the lay elders of the church and charged them with the necessity of healing this parasitic conflict in our bloodstream as a church. We began to pray for both women, refusing to take sides. Then we developed a strategy of working with each of them. We talked, encouraged, and exhorted each of them. It took hours of listening and loving with both of them until the wounds were cleaned of the infection of judgments and distrust. Then it was time to bring them face to face. Both of them now realized that their relationship was debilitating the church and that they could no longer go on the way they were. After many times of confrontation, the sting was gone and they opened channels of love to each other again. One night at a church supper they both stood together and shared the new life they had found in Christ and with each other.

I can think of many other similar instances. In each case, however, it took a concerned wound healer who would not stand by idly with reserved aloofness. Wound healing is everyone's obligation and responsibility.

Paul reminded these Christians of Philippi that there were tremendous resources available for healing relationships. He helped them to remember that they were co-workers, yokefellows of the gospel. What they believed about Christ and his forgiveness was ample power for healing their differences. He then helps them to know that they all belong to Christ, whose "names are in God's book of the living." They are real Christians in spite of their bickerings. The living Spirit of Christ himself would be the motivating, effective power of healing between them. He was and is the wound healer for eternity and can use us as his instruments, agents of reconciliation.

Recently, I was asked the question, "Where in your life is God saying, 'The next move is yours'?" I hear the same question now. What is my next move as a wound healer? What's yours?

> Lord, I feel that you have laid two things on me today. First, I want to consider my relationships. "Where do I need healing with someone else?" Help me to make the first move today. Then I hear you saying, "Who needs you to step in and bridge the gap?" Show me the way, Lord! Amen.

Rejoice Anyhow!

WHEN THINGS ARE DIFFICULT AND SEEM IMPOSSIBLE, REJOICE!

May the Lord give you joy always. I say it again, rejoice! (Phil. 4:4).

Blaise Pascal, the philosopher-mathematician, had an experience that changed the course of his life. Pascal wrote out the experience and sewed it into his clothes. It was found on his body when he died nine years later. What he had written went like this: "The year of the Lord 1654. Monday, 23 November, from about half past ten in the evening until about half past twelve at night: fire. God of Abraham, God of Isaac, God of Jacob, not the God of philosophers and scholars. Certainty, joy, peace.

135

God of Jesus Christ, He is only found along the ways that are taught in the gospel. Tears of joy. I had parted from Him. Let me never be separated from Him. Surrender to Jesus Christ." [9]

This experience, so eloquently recorded, sustained Pascal. Each time he would falter, he would touch the portion of his coat containing the record of his experience and rejoice again. Note the progression: Certainty, Joy, Peace. That's the way it happens for all of us. The certainty of Christ's unchanging love, the outburst of joy, the inner mood of peace.

Paul had found that certainty which enabled him to rejoice in all circumstances. We read today's verse with amazement. Paul is in prison, a death sentence hangs over him, concern for the churches besets him, and yet he says, "Rejoice!"

This is more than a passing parenthesis in Paul's advice to his friends in Philippi. Actually he is giving his cherished fellow Christians a secret of how to live in problems, difficulties, and frustrations. He knew of the dangers ahead for the church everywhere. He was not being flippantly pious with easy advice. Instead, he was helping them to discover an aspect of their nature which could liberate them when things got tough.

If I were to transcribe a verse and sew it into my clothing, it would be this one from Philippians 4:4. The one thing I wish I could give as a gift to the people I love would be the remedial power of this verse.

Here's the secret of victorious living Paul's words unlocked for me. When things get tough or difficult or downright impossible—rejoice. I have found that the same emotional channels which can contain and transmit discouragement and despair can be used for praise. When I surrender a particularly troublesome time, dare to thank God for it, and rejoice that he will use it for my ultimate good, I find that my attention is shifted from all the bad eventualities to God's possibilities. I know one thing for sure: God is faithful, nothing is ever so bad that his good cannot be brought out of it. I agree with Albert Einstein when he said, "I shall never believe that God plays dice with the world."

The transition point from discouragement to encouragement for me is in rejoicing. The more persistently I rejoice, the more my emotions are shifted away from the outward manifestation of tragedy to the inward movement of God's Spirit. Just as discouragement is contagious, so, too, rejoicing is creatively infectious. Years of experimentation have trained my emotions to move more quickly to praise. My motto, based on this verse, is "Regardless . . . Rejoice!"

Paul's admonition is a grammatical imperative. It is not a pleasant suggestion he makes just in case some of the Philippians might want to use it. It's a command. Rejoice in the Lord always. Then as Paul considers the power of praise in problems, he reiterates for undeniable emphasis, "Again I say, rejoice!"

I find that rejoicing opens me not only to the possibility of God's intervention but frees me for the invasion of His Spirit. All great prayer, all liberating worship, all lasting encounters with God, begin with praise and rejoicing.

Paul challenges us to habitually rejoice until the inadvertent gear into which we shift when under pressure is one of praise. It has been said that for some people religion is like an artificial limb. It has neither warmth nor life; and although it helps them stumble along, it never becomes a part of them—it must be strapped on each day. That's just the opposite of what Paul's talking about. When we persistently rejoice, we become open to God and open to what he can do with our lives. Praise is not a luxury of spiritual moods, it's the latch which unlocks the prison of discouragement.

Last week, I had one of those negative days in which everyone and everything I dealt with was down. The meetings I attended, the people I counseled, the problems I tried to solve, all infused depressing feelings into me. It was a blue Monday and a black Friday crammed together to produce a restless Wednesday. As the day proceeded, I forgot about the wisdom of this verse. By the end of the day my psyche felt like a punching bag with the stuffing knocked out. I took a long walk before I went to bed. Paul's words in today's verse came back to me, and I realized that it was not just that day or the people in it, but I had forgotten to continually praise God throughout the day. I walked and thought, trying to put myself together. Each ten steps, I thought of something for which I could rejoice. Soon I was singing praises. After each thing for which I gave thanks,

I would say "Praise God!" My pace quickened as my mood shifted. The computer of my being had new data and I could feel the surge of emotions of joy and peace. I went to bed and slept in the everlasting arms of a gracious God.

> O God, I thank you for my emotions. With them I can feel life to the fullest. But you know how my feelings get burdened down with the impressions of human need without the expression of praise. Open my eyes to your great goodness and providing care. I trust you Lord, and claim the promise that you will be with me always. So, now and all through this day, I wait to rejoice in you while I live in my circumstances. Accept my rejoicing praise now as I review the specific people and situations for which I can rejoice immediately so that eventually I can rejoice in all things. Amen.

What To Do When People Fail Us

LET'S EXPRESS OUR ATTITUDES TO ONE ANOTHER AS IF THE LORD'S RETURN WERE TODAY.

Show a gentle attitude toward all. The Lord is coming soon (Phil. 4:5).

The other evening I heard John Claypool tell a wonderful story which had profound implications for me. A young boy told about a time when his teacher had to leave the classroom for a time. He asked his students to stay in their places and study what he had taught them. The time he was away stretched out longer than expected. The children did not do as he had asked, but were so concerned about his return that they stationed sentinels to announce his return. They spent all their energy watching for his return and accomplished very little while he was away.

We can all remember those hiatuses of hilarity while our teachers stepped out of the room. We can also recall how hard we tried to pretend that we had been working diligently when he returned.

The church has been something like those children in its expectation of the Lord's return in the Second Coming. There are Christians in every age whose concern for the Eschaton has been so intense that they have had little time for the work Christ has left for us to do. Some Christians actually get fanatic about the end times and think of little else.

I believe in the Lord who came, who comes to us now as abiding Savior, and the Lord of creation who will come again. All three aspects are essential. I am thankful that our history will some day come to an end and Christ shall reign. The "rapture" which we will know at his return, I anticipate with expectation. But the study of last things should never block out our daily obedience to follow Christ now.

I am interested in Paul's challenge to the Philippians in today's verse. He does not say, "The Lord is coming, therefore forget your obligations, don't finish college, don't worry about the conditions in which people live in society, don't share the faith, and don't be concerned about fellowship of the church!" Nor did he say, "Study to find out the exact day or week, find out where he will return and go there and wait until he appears."

Rather, Paul says, "Show a gentle attitude toward all. The Lord is coming soon." The words in Greek which are translated, "Gentle attitude," can also be translated forbearance, winsomeness, sweet reasonableness. Further investigation of the words reveals they were used for one who lives the fullness of the law but applies it with tender, empathetical justice. This kind of person is not harsh or judgmental, but longs for the ultimate good of people for whom he is responsible.

The hardest time to be gentle is when we know we are right and someone else is obviously dead wrong. It is equally difficult to be gracious when we hold professional or personal power over others. It's so easy to be harsh and unbending. When

139

we are, it's a sure sign of our own insecurity. But the greatest temptation for most of us is when someone has failed us or himself has admitted it, and his destiny or happiness is in our hands. We hold the power to give or refuse a blessing.

Recently, a dear friend hurt me in both word and action. Each time we met, the tarnished relationship expressed its dullness. I had that juicy relish of being misused and misunderstood. I almost began to enjoy the leverage of being the offended one. His first overtures of restitution were resisted because of the gravity of the judgment I had made. He had taken a key idea I had shared with him in confidence and had developed it as his own before I had a chance to use it. The plagiarism of ideas had been coupled with the use of some of my written material, reproduced under his name.

Now, how's that for a justified case against a friend in the Lord? I should have every right to hang him by his thumbs, shouldn't I? What would Paul say about that?

Exactly what he said to the Philippians. In fact it was today's verse which finally got through to me some months ago. I realized that however right I might be, the spiritual need of this brother was most crucial. The most difficult thing was to surrender my pique and work through the hurt. He felt as badly as I did.

But the thing which liberated me was the idea Paul stresses here, "The Lord is coming soon." Life is short. I will be dealt with by God for my failures also. Finally, the Lord got me where he wanted me: to deal with this man as he had dealt with me when I consciously failed him and the people I love. For a brief time, I felt the gentleness of the Lord, that sweet mixture of justice and grace. His word to me was clear and undeniable, "Lloyd, why is it so important to you who gets the credit, just so my work gets done?" I gave up my right to be what only God could be as this man's judge and savior. The gentle attitude began to flow.

I have shared this story with you only to show that to exposit the Word of God means we must live it, reluctant cooperators with God though we may be at times.

What about you? Have you ever faced something like that in

your life? How about right now—in your marriage, with your children, with your friends, at work, or in the church?

> Lord, we thank you that indeed you are coming soon. May true realization of that intensify our desire to do the work you have given us to do. Particularly bring to our minds people who need your gentle attitude expressed through us. When we are right, Lord, it's so difficult to be gracious. Bring to our minds right now the memory of how you have dealt with us when we have failed you and give us freedom to be nothing less to others. Amen.

Prayer Begins With God

ASK GOD ONCE; THANK HIM WITHOUT CEASING THAT HE HAS HEARD.

Don't worry about anything, but in all your prayers ask God for what you need, always asking him with a thankful heart (Phil. 4:6).

Something has happened to my praying lately. The more I have studied this verse along with 1 John 5:13–15, the more I have prayed differently and with greater satisfaction. Paul and John are in agreement about an aspect of prayer which has blown my mind and revolutionized my experience of prayer. Here's what John says, "I write you this so that you may know that you have eternal life—you who believe in the name of the Son of God. This is why we have courage in God's presence; we are sure that he will hear us if we ask him for anything that is according to his will."

These verses communicate several crucial discoveries about prayer for me.

141

The first is *prayer begins with God*. Our prayers are not to beg for God's attention. Our desire to pray is the result of his Spirit working within us to motivate us to pray for the very things he is more ready to give than we are to ask. He created us for relationship with him. There are dimensions of his love and care which he wills not to give us until he has initiated the need and desire within us. The main point of Jesus' parables on prayer about the supportive, persistent friend asking for bread at midnight, the indefatigable widow ceaselessly besieging the judge, and the father and his gifts to his children is that God is more ready to give what we need than we are as human beings to one another. Jesus' admonition to ask, seek, and knock in prayer (Luke 11:9, 10) is clarification of our part in the process which begins and is stimulated by God himself. This changes our attitude entirely. Prayer begins with God, sweeps into the heart of man and returns to God.

The second thing this leads me to is that praying *is to receive the mind of Christ*. So often when we pray we feel that we must convince God that something is best for us or for the people for whom we pray. "This is why we have courage in God's presence (praying); we are *sure* that he will hear us *if* we ask him for anything that is according to *his* will." Now that's a great "if," and this condition is experienced as we pray to discern the will of God so that what we ask for is already part of his plan for us. That means our praying will be more listening than talking and less filled with repetitious requests, as if he did not hear us the first time.

That leads to the third aspect: *Prayer is for giving thanks*. Paul says, "Don't worry, ask God for what you need . . . and then . . . always asking him with a thankful heart." We ask for what he has guided us to ask in keeping with his will. After that we give thanks that he has heard us and the matter is being worked out according to his timing, planning, and purpose. I used to ask, worry, and ask again as if God were hard of hearing. Now I am trying to learn how to ask once and thank him repeatedly.

All of this is climaxed in the realization that prayer is guided by God's nature. He is the same yesterday, today, and tomorrow. The same love he revealed on Calvary is as real at this moment as it was when Jesus died for us because "God so loved the world." He has created us in such a way that we can discern his direction and have the boldness to pray for it to happen in our lives.

But wait! How can we be so sure we know his will? Couldn't we manipulate that to be simply our extension of what we want? Strange, isn't it, that we immediately think that what he wants could never be what we want. Or, if we want something to happen, we think it's a sure thing that it's not what God wants. Why do we mistrust ourselves so severely? Haven't we asked him to come and live in us? He's faithful to his promise that he would "make his home in us." "Christ in you, the hope of glory."

But we do have some safeguards. He will never guide us contrary to his word revealed in the life, message, and ministry of his Son. Is what we feel guided to pray for consistent with Jesus Christ? Is it the loving thing, ultimately, for all concerned? Will it bring us closer to him and be compatible with his kingdom? Beyond these check points, I think we can dare to trust our thinking and feelings as surrendered to him and obedient to his motivation and molding.

Dag Hammarskjöld wrote in *Markings*, "The more faithfully you listen to the voice within you, the better you will hear what is sounding outside."

I suggest that you memorize the two Scriptures we've talked about right now. Let them become part of you. Brood over them today. Mull them over and ask God to reveal to you how to pray in the light of the truth they contain.

The other day I felt led to ask God about my schedule. He put my involvements on my mind. I tried to spread out all that I am doing before him. As I lingered in his presence, I felt led to pray about certain aspects of my program. I felt an impelling desire to excuse myself from several things I was doing. For a whole week I acted as if I were going to change my commitments of time in several areas. God had ample time to change my feelings. Then I followed through with some resignations from activities in certain boards and organizations. One was particularly hard to let go of. But as I did it, I felt a surge of assurance. Later on, with the decks cleared, I was given an opportunity to do something I have longed to do for years. But once again, back to prayer to talk to God about what he had motivated me to discuss with him. The same period of trial ensued. Then a burst of liberated feelings. I felt "right" about doing what he had prepared long before I had the thought or inclination to pray about it.

William James was right when he said, "We and God have business with each other; and in opening ourselves to his influence our deepest destiny is fulfilled."

> Holy Father, we are your guests in this conversation. You opened the dialogue with your instigating Spirit. Lord, bring to our consciousness the things you want to do business about today. Give me the freedom to trust your Spirit in me and the boldness to ask for those things you have guided me to know that you are more ready to give than I am to ask. Amen.

Peace We Cannot Contrive

THERE IS A DEEP, INNER PEACE WHICH IS INCONSISTENT WITH THE CIRCUMSTANCES IN WHICH WE FIND OURSELVES AND UNASSAILABLE BY ANY MOOD OR FEELING.

And God's peace, which is far beyond human understanding, will keep your hearts and minds safe, in Christ Jesus (Phil. 4:7).

Today, I want you to join me in getting in touch with our real feelings. Deep down in your inner self, do you feel at peace? Do you feel an imperturbable peace inside which no memory,

144

broken relationship, worry, or fear can disturb? As you sit quietly, what is it which robs you of truly being tranquil inside your own heart? External pressures? Demanding people and situations in today's plans? Hopes for the future devouring the present? Insecurities gnawing at a sense of well being?

Edward Sheldon, the outstanding playwright, experienced peace in spite of crippling arthritis, which in its latter stages left him totally blind. His biography, *The Man Who Lived Twice*, is about his discovery which has moved and inspired so many. He exposed an extraordinary courage and faith which enabled him to triumph over almost impossible afflictions. "I never felt the need of a definite religion until recently. I used to think I could stand up to anything that came along, but I don't anymore." The biographer picked up the story and told that, "During the next weeks Sheldon came to grips with destiny and from some hidden reservoir of the spirit drew strength to go on. He not only found the courage to endure under a blight from which death might have seemed a welcome release, but he formed the sure belief that affliction could not destroy the purpose of his life. In the moment of crises he found a faith which would not only sustain him in the thirty remaining years of his life but which would reach out in powerful and mysterious ways into the lives of other people." [10]

The hidden reservoir of the spirit! That's the kind of peace that Paul is talking about in this verse. There is a peace of God which passes understanding. That does not mean that we cannot comprehend it. But it does mean that the true peace which comes from God is so penetrating and permanent and persistent that man's mind, with all its skill and all its knowledge and comprehension, can never contrive it or totally explore its riches. It is utterly beyond our ability to produce for ourselves. It is God's gift; it is not man's contriving. There is only one way to know this peace: to take all that we have and are, all whom we love and all they mean, all that we have been or ever hope to be, all that we yearn that life will produce, and to place them under the complete control and care of our Lord. That quality of trust produces this kind of peace. Christian peace is neither the calm of inactivity nor the mere passive enjoyment of freedom from strife. It is Christ's gift in the midst of strife and turmoil. "Peace I leave with you; my peace I give to you; not as the world gives do I give to you. Let not your hearts be troubled, neither let them be afraid" (John 14:27, RSV).

Paul tells the Philippians that this kind of peace will keep their minds and hearts in Christ Jesus. This is very significant. The word for "keep" means guard, protect, garrison about, patrol around. The peace of God will surround the mind and heart and keep worry and fear away. This is exciting to consider because it means that we can know an imperturbable peace in the midst of very difficult, disturbing circumstances and surroundings. This peace guards the thoughts of the mind and the feelings of the heart. It abides—whatever happens.

This is because of the three ingredients of true peace as it is clarified in Scripture. First, it means forgiveness of past sins and failures. "He has delivered us from the dominion of darkness and transferred us to the kingdom of his beloved Son, in whom we have redemption, the forgiveness of sins. For in him all the fulness of God was pleased to dwell, and through him to reconcile to himself all things, whether on earth or in heaven, making peace by the blood of the cross" (Col. 1:13, 19, RSV).

Secondly, it means freedom. "Now the Lord is the Spirit, and where the Spirit of the Lord is, there is freedom. And we all, with unveiled face, beholding the glory of the Lord, are being changed into his likeness from one degree of glory to another; for this comes from the Lord who is the Spirit" (2 Cor. 3:17, RSV).

Thirdly, peace arises out of reconciled relationships. "For he is our peace, who has made us both one, and has broken down the dividing wall of hostility, by abolishing in his flesh the law of commandments and ordinances, that he might create in himself one new man in place of the two, so making peace" (Eph. 2:14, 15, RSV). Paul's admonition to the Colossians was, "And let the peace of Christ rule in your hearts, to which indeed you were called in the one body" (Col. 3:15, RSV).

This kind of peace comes from a continuing discovery of the Lordship of Christ in our lives and affairs. He put it bluntly: "Do you suppose that I have come to give peace on earth? No I tell you, but rather division." He cuts into any area of life which has the potential of dissuading our complete dependence on him and absolute loyalty to his plan for us. This helps us: We can know that any time we feel disturbed, guilty, or ill at ease there is something the surgery of his sword is beginning to cut. Peace should be the continuing experience of our inner lives. If not, then something is wrong which must be dealt with immediately. Jesus did not come to provide the peace of the world, but the unimpeachable control of his Spirit around us and within us.

The peace which passes understanding is inseparable from justice. You cannot plan to have peace. It comes as a result of righteous justice in our lives. When something is wrong in our relationships or in our daily life, there will be little peace.

The other day a man said to me, "I had slept about three hours when I was awakened. I have never felt Christ so close. But he was not there to comfort only, but to show me myself and to help me understand my distorted feelings about a situation in which I had felt hurt and hostility. By the time he finished with me, I knew why I had felt so little peace lately. When I accepted what he had to say to me, a limitless flood of peace flowed into my feelings again." The absence of peace is an alarming danger signal that something's wrong.

A trusted friend whom I admire very much said that he had had dinner with a group of new Christians. Their spontaneity and joy altered him to the need of a fresh touch of God's Spirit in his life. He prayed for that as he went to sleep. The next day was different, and he felt the peace which he had lost return in fresh flow. Sometimes, the evidence of the power of Christ in others will alert us to how drab and unadventuresome our lives have become. That realization is the cut of the sword of our Lord to prepare us for a deeper experience of his peace. It is Christ's gift when we are able to say, as one man put it, "I am often astonished to discover that deep inside I am at peace, while everything around me is in a state of hectic, nervous agitation."

Our prayer for today is one that Thomas à Kempis prayed: "Lord Jesus, let Thy will be mine, and let my will always follow Thine, and agree perfectly therewith. . . . Grant that I may rest in Thee above all things that can be desired, and that my heart may be at peace in Thee. Thou art the true peace of the heart, Thou art its only rest; out of Thee all things are irksome and restless. In this very peace which is in Thee, the one Supreme Good, I will sleep and take my rest. . . ." Amen.

"Well, What Do You Think?"

WE CAN LOVE GOD WITH OUR MINDS.

In conclusion, my brothers, fill your minds with those things that are good and deserve praise: things that are true, noble, right, pure, lovely, and honorable. Put into practice what you learned and received from me, both from my words and from my deeds. And the God who gives us peace will be with you (Phil. 4:8, 9).

"Well, what do you think?" This is a question we often ask in daily conversation when we want a person's opinion about a particular subject. But the question needs to be asked on a much deeper level. What we think about shapes what we are and become. "As he thinketh in his heart, so is he" (Prov. 23:7, KJV). The quality of our thoughts affects what we feel and how we handle life. Confused, distorted, or mushy thinking will be manifested in our health, our relationships, and our productivity. We hear a lot today about thinking being a "head trip," as if that were bad. But what's going on in our minds will determine the effectiveness and lasting value of all else that happens to us. Irenaeus said that "the glory of God is man fully alive." I believe that includes our thinking. We have said that the gospel is

148

not just ideas, but relationships. That's true for a much needed emphasis, but the gospel must reorient and transform our ideas about life, ourselves, the world, and God himself.

Paul concludes his delineation (Phil. 4:1–9) of how to stand firm in our life in the Lord with today's verse which is a plea to fill our minds with thoughts which will guide the formulation of Christlikeness in our whole character. He is urgently concerned about what is going on in the inner chambers of our minds. The private thoughts, the fetishes which form our values, the fantasies which either enable or dissolve us, and the dreams which focus our hopes and goals can either be mind-shaped prisons or thoughts running to freedom.

In William Hulme's *I Hate To Bother You, But . . .*, there is a telling conversation. " 'I hate to say this, but sometimes I get to wondering if there is a God—and it scares me! . . . Maybe I think too much—I don't know,' he said. 'How do you mean?' I asked. 'Oh, if I would just quit thinking about these things—you know how God can hear everybody's prayers at the same time and how a dead person can live again—things like that?' 'Have you tried to quit thinking about these things?' 'Yes, I guess I have,' he said." [11]

Paul would not agree. He would say, "Go on thinking and let God convert your mind." He gives the Philippians a six-way test of how to fill our minds with things which are good and deserve praise. What he suggests is not only a good basis for thought-cleaning but for the basis of creative decisions. Here are the questions to ask about our thoughts.

First, is it true? This does not mean veracious or truthful, but consistent with what something is in its essential nature. We have irrational thoughts which are a distortion of reality. They confuse us because we build our understanding on an unstable foundation. For the Christian the question is, "Is my perception of something realistic in the light of the gospel?" Jules Renard said, "God does not believe in our god." We can be so inconsistent with Jesus' revelation that our thinking about God and life can be conceptually contradictory. Kierkegaard was right, "We need to introduce Christianity to Christendom." The more we are steeped in the message and life of our Lord, the more true our thinking will be. This frees us of the dicta of inherited cultural misconceptions about life.

Next, is it noble? This means, "venerable, inviting reverence, worthy of reverence." Does a thought we have produce reverence? There are thoughts about God and his beautiful signature in the people and natural beauty around us which develops nobility of character in us. Whenever I begin prayer or worship thinking about some aspect or revealed nature of God, my feelings are transformed. When I think of people as gifts of God, I treat them differently. When I contemplate the serendipities of God, my possibility level is heightened. The thought that God loves me just as I am liberates my thinking about myself and others.

For example, consider how this works in the sexual realm of our thoughts. Reverence for the sexuality of another person frees us from making someone a thing and not a person. The eroticism of our day is enjoyment without responsibility for the whole person. A woman told me that she was propositioned for an affair with no strings attached. She was prepared by years of noble thoughts about really caring for people. "I love you too much to do that," she responded and went on to explain that as much as she enjoyed her friend's attention, she could not use him in a brief encounter without the lasting care and concern of marriage. What erotic thoughts keep you from nobility in Christ?

Then we can ask, "Is it right?" This means just or righteous. Sin is anything which separates us from God or any other person. Righteousness is not following a set of rules but being in relationship. Do our thoughts contribute to the growth of our relationship with God and the people of our lives? We have been made righteous through faith in Christ. What if our thoughts disturb that? When we respond to the dicta of having to do something to make God love us, we begin a chain of thought which results in self-righteousness. A friend of mine confessed, "I preach grace but I live the law." His thinking is that there is always something more we must do to please God. Recently, he had a heart attack from overwork in the ministry. His overwork pattern was based on false thinking ingrained by his father that God loves not the cheerful giver but the overextended hard worker. Now he has been given a second chance at life, and his "right" thinking about God's acceptance has freed him to get as much accomplished—motivated by praise, not pressure. What unrighteous thoughts keep you from enjoying a right relationship with people or God?

Paul moves on to, "Is it pure?" The thoughts which are pure are those which are not confused by distortions of untruth inconsistent with the gospel. Recently a friend filled his pool with city water. It was a murky green. "You mean I drink that water?" I asked. I was assured that it was safe. Then as we added purifying chemicals to the water, it became crystal clear. The filtering system keeps it that way. I thought of the purifying system my thoughts need to free me to act creatively. Jesus Christ is like those cleansing chemicals in my mind. When I pump thoughts through the filters of the gospel, I am amazed at how much clearer my thinking is about life.

Closely related is the next test, "Is it lovely?" That is, does it excite love and produce loveable action? There are thoughts which produce loving relationships and motivate loving concern. The best generator of this quality of thought is contemplation of the way God loves us. When we are overcome with the thought of undeserved, unearned love through the cross, we think and express love more freely. That's why a study and reflection of the gospel reforms our thought life. We can never think too much about the grace of God. I learned this again on a retreat I attended recently. There was nothing new that I had not heard before, but we studied, meditated, and witnessed about the cross. I went home and back to work a new man, filled with the lovely thoughts of God's amazing love. My life was different because I was different. All thoughts were screened through the liberating question, "Is it the loving thing? Is it consistent with the cross?"

The last test is, "Is it honorable?" *The Expositor's Greek Testament* translates this as, "Whatever excellence there be, or fit object of praise." That forces the questions, "Are my thought patterns worthy of our Lord's praise? Are they excellent by his standard of what is constructive for our thought life? What would we do with our thought habits if we gave him control

151

of our minds?" He knows what helps and heals and what hurts and hinders. That leaves us with the question, "Have we ever committed our thought life to our Lord?"

The other day I was asked the question with which we began this meditation. After I had given my opinion, the deeper question lingered with repetitious persistence. Just how do I use the gift of thinking? It led to some penetrating reevaluation. How would you answer?

Lord, thank you for the gift of my mind. I can think in such a way as to grow in Christ or my thoughts can be a conflicting contradiction. I yield my mind to the six-way test Paul has given me. Help me to be open for you to change my mind! Amen.

Situational Strength

WE CAN DO ALL THINGS THROUGH CHRIST
WHO STRENGTHENS US!

How great is the joy I have in my life in the Lord! . . . I have learned to be satisfied with what I have. I know what it is to be in need, and what it is to have more than enough. I have learned this secret, so that anywhere, at any time, I am content, whether I am full or hungry, whether I have too much or too little. I have the strength to face all conditions by the power that Christ gives me (Phil. 4:10–13).

Peter Drucker has a challenging word about taking risks. He says that there are essentially four kinds of risks: the risk one must accept; the risk one can afford to take; the risk one cannot afford to take; the risk one cannot afford not to take.

Paul's life in Christ had been filled with the last category. His biography could be entitled, "Risky Christianity." It was risky not in the sense of being a poor investment, but in being one constant risk of safety and comfort for the sake of Christ. He always ventured beyond the comfortable territory of security and ease to the adventuresome frontiers of a risky life. It had not been easy as he recorded himself: "I have been in prison . . . I have been whipped . . . and I have been near death. . . . Five times I was given thirty-nine lashes by the Jews; three times I was whipped by the Romans, and once I was stoned; I have been in three shipwrecks, and once I spent twenty-four hours in the water. In my many travels I have been in danger from fellow Jews and from Gentiles; there have been dangers in cities, dangers in the wilds, dangers on the high seas, and dangers from false friends. There has been work and toil; often I have gone without sleep; I have been hungry and thirsty; and I have often been without enough food, shelter, or clothing. And, not to mention other things, every day I am under the pressure of my concern for all the churches. When someone is weak, then I feel weak too; when someone falls into sin, I am filled with distress" (2 Cor. 11:23–29).

Quite a ministry! Indeed, Paul had learned to be in need. There was no cost too great for the spread of the gospel. Christ himself was the reason for this. In him, there was constantly a risk Paul could not (to use Drucker's words) afford not to take. The double negative gives stirring emphasis.

But notice, he also survived having more than enough. That's a risk of another kind. Success can be harder to take than difficulties. False security can award us with an arm chair to rock away the rest of our lives in satisfied recapitulation of old battles and triumphs. I am convinced that prosperity is more difficult to handle than troublesome times. When we're up against it, we know there's no hope but in Christ. But affluence and prosperity in either spiritual or material riches can make us like an old college athletic hero who wears his letter sweater everywhere but in the shower.

Paul gives us the secret of risky Christianity. "I have learned the secret so that anywhere, at any time, I am content." "Content" means to be full. It was originally used for the feeding of animals. A fattened or satisfied animal was described this way. Paul was content because he had the most life could offer: the love of Christ, a sense of effectiveness in sharing the gospel, the fellowship of fellow Christians, and a mission which electrified life with challenging excitement. Neither discomfort nor distinguishing accomplishments could ever replace that contentment.

No wonder Paul could say, "I have the strength to face all conditions by the power Christ gives me." That was the source of his daring.

I believe we have failed contemporary Christians in the church by not making Christianity risky enough. Many of us long for a costly challenge to demand a risk. The churches in America which are growing are those which make a significant demand for people's commitment.

The people in our church in Hollywood who are discovering the adventure of Christ are those who are risking the security of the familiar and daring to be vulnerable in loving people, aggressive in following Christ's guidance in their finances, and involved in fearless witness to Christ's power. It's not safe, but neither will they be sorry.

It's dangerous to generalize. My risk may not be yours. But I must take mine as God reveals it. The question is, "If we dare to risk, will God see us through?" Paul knew from experience that he would. So say I!

For some, the risk is in being open and free with people. Others will find risk in being completely honest with their mates. Some will faithfully tithe and write the first check for the Lord. Others will begin to talk about what they believe when rejection or ridicule may result. There will be some who will dare to change jobs and do the thing they have felt guided to do for years. Restitutions will be made and old wounds healed. New ventures will be started for Christ and old habits will be committed to his liberating power. The examples are limitless.

This hits me personally. Most of my ventures in spreading the gospel have been underwritten financially by churches or organizations. Recently I felt led to join four friends in Christ to sponsor a series of conferences across the nation which we felt were desperately needed. It meant obligating myself not just to speak but to pay the bill. As a child of the Depression, I am very cautious financially. If I ever worry, it's about financial security. The risk was real, but the rewards for Christ in America can be beyond calculation. Beyond my tithes and savings, I had to trust God that I would be able to meet my obligation for the conferences.

Business men in my congregation go through this all the time. For many of them it would not be a risk, but another investment venture. For me, it was a real risk, but it was delicious to be stretched out with no visible means of support. But the invisible . . . ah Christ!

I have tried to illustrate that there is a risk for all of us which we "cannot afford not to take." What's yours?

> Lord Jesus, I want to know what the risk would be for me. What am I to do that would really stretch my faith? I know I cannot live on another man's risk or live vicariously through another person's daring. I know that I will be content whether I have too much or too little. Thank you, Lord. Amen.

Needs And Wants

GOD WILL PROVIDE ALL OUR NEEDS AND REDEEM OUR WANTS ACCORDING TO HIS PLAN FOR US.

But it was very good of you to help me in my troubles. You Philippians yourselves know very well that when I left Macedonia, in the early days of preaching the Good News, you were the only church to help me; you were the only ones who shared my profits and losses.

More than once, when I needed help in Thessalonica, you sent it to me. It is not that I just want to receive gifts; rather, I want to see profit added to your account. Here, then, is my receipt for everything you have given me—and it has been more than enough! I have all I need, now that Epaphroditus has brought me all your gifts. These are like a sweet-smelling offering to God, a sacrifice which is acceptable and pleasing to him. And my God, with all his abundant wealth in Christ Jesus, will supply all your needs. To our God and Father be the glory for ever and ever. Amen (Phil. 4:14–20).

There's a great difference between wants and needs. We may not need what we want, and what we want may not be needed for our good. This whole passage deals with needs, not wants. Paul's needs were met by the gifts of the Philippians. They sent him no luxuries, only the necessities to keep his ministry going. His gratitude is expressed in very symbolic accountant's language. They shared his profits and losses. He wanted profit added to their spiritual ledger for what they had done. His letter is a receipt of thanksgiving. Their gifts were like the sweet smell of a sacrifice to God. What a beautiful image! Anything we do for each other in the fellowship is an offering to God. We cannot give to the church. We are the church! All that we have belongs to God and therefore to each other in times of need. That pleases God. Think of what would happen to the finances of the church if we were motivated by that joyous generosity and didn't need Every Member Canvasses, slick brochures, and emotional appeals for money.

Paul's gift in response is a prayer. He tapped into the one limitless resource, the wealth of Jesus Christ, and prayed that all of their needs would be supplied. Their needs were not financial but spiritual. They needed courage, the forgiving love to unite their church, power to affect Philippi with the gospel. That's the reason Paul could make this almost unbelievable promise. Because they had given out, God could put in. They were channels which could experience the flow of fresh reserves from God because they had opened themselves in gracious outpouring. This would be hard to accept by those who believe that what they have achieved they did on their own strength, or those who have held on tenaciously to themselves and their love —afraid to give either. When we give ourselves away to the point of our own discomfort, then the limitless wealth of God in his own Spirit, the problems he solves for us, the resources he untaps, and the people he gives us are a cause for amazement and unlimited praise.

There are times when our wants are satisfied before the needs of others. To be a channel of the wealth of Jesus Christ is to feel the needs of others as if they were our own. That's what made the giving practices of the Philippian church so remarkable. Whose needs are being denied because of the willful fulfillment of our wants?

But also, like a human father's love multiplied incalculably, our Father is conscious of our wants as well as our needs. He is tenderly conscious of our secret wishes and fondest dreams. He is not against the creative enjoyments we long for. We can talk to him about the longings of our hearts and know that he will provide what is best for us.

I remember when I was a young pastor struggling to start a new church. I needed a rest, but there was no money for a vacation. I told God about my need and my wants. One day after church a man slipped two plane tickets and a vacation hotel reservation into my pocket. The note said, "Just because we love God and you." That was difficult to receive because of all of my needs at that time. The money could have been used for other needs in my life. I tried to explain to the man and return the tickets. I will never forget his response, "You both need and want a vacation. It's okay. Have a frolic to the glory of God."

Since then I have unashamedly told God about both my needs and my wants. He provides the one and redeems the other according to what is best for me.

Lord God, Paul has given me a picture of sharing and mutuality in the true Christian fellowship which challenges me. Today in this prayer, I spread all of my

157

needs out before you. I want to want what you want for me. Out of the abundant wealth of Jesus Christ, supply all my needs today. Amen.

Bother Us, We Can Cope

THERE'S POWER AVAILABLE FOR FAITHFUL-NESS IN THE SYSTEM.

Greetings to all God's people who belong to Christ Jesus. The brothers here with me send you their greetings. All God's people here send greetings, especially those who belong to the Emperor's palace. May the grace of the Lord Jesus Christ be with you all (Phil. 4:21–23).

Vinnette Carroll's musical "Don't Bother Me, I Can't Cope" is a rich slice of Americana. The evening I saw it performed at the Huntington Hartford Theater in Hollywood, I felt the audience galvanized together in a catalytic experience of communication. None of us was prepared for the wallop the title song had on our evading excuses for being involved and responsible for people and our society. The singers would belt out the crises which grip our culture and then would be interrupted by the refrain which cut like a sharp knife, "But don't bother me, I can't cope."

When I left the theater, the words kept running through my mind. Then I thought of the church. How often in our nation's crises we have said, "Don't bother us, we can't cope!"

The more I thought about it, the more I realized that our theme song should be just the opposite, "Bother us, we can cope!" We can say that because Christ can cope with all our troubles and the problems of our society if we will allow him to use us. Maybe a better way to put it would be, "Bother us, Christ can cope through us."

That night when I read my Bible, I came across Paul's prayer for the church in Ephesus. There was the power to cope! "I

158

ask God, from the wealth of his glory, to give you power through his Spirit to be strong in your inner selves, and that Christ will make his home in your hearts, through faith. I pray that you may have your roots and foundations in love, and that you, together with all God's people, may have the power to understand how broad and long and high and deep is Christ's love . . . . and so be completely filled with the perfect fulness of God" (Eph. 3:16–19).

In our concluding Scripture from Philippians Paul makes a reference which is almost lost in the flourish of the finish to his epistle and the benediction. He says, "The brothers here with me send you their greetings, especially those who belong to the Emperor's palace." The Emperor's palace! Can you imagine what it must have been like to cope as a Christian there? Servants, converted soldiers, and political personnel who belonged to Christ had to live out their faith in that pagan, power-driven, man-exalting regime. It was not easy to be Christ's person while caught in the system.

Nor has it ever been. Today Christians live and work in institutions which often contradict and sometimes confuse their witness to Christ. We all must earn a living wage. There are times when our beliefs are stifled by policies and practices which are contrary to what we believe. It's difficult to cope. Sometimes people are less important than policies.

Whenever people gather together to produce a product, provide education, or promote a commodity there must be organization. The structure of that organization can debilitate the very people it exists to help. There are universities which become impersonal, churches which contradict the gospel they proclaim, governments that are no longer in touch with the populace.

What does a Christian do? How does he cope?

One word in Paul's last sentence gives us the answer: grace. It is by grace, God's unmerited favor, that we win the battle of being faithful without losing the war of being effective. If we ask him, he will give us people in our structures with whom we can share the delight of being alive in Christ, and also by grace, he will give us decision-making power to influence the lives of others. We are to keep free of giving our allegiance to the wrong gods by continually surrendering the difficult surroundings to him and anticipating and receiving the great things he will do.

I for one want to live out my faith in the real world as it is with the power of Christ. You may want to join the chorus of life-affirming, structure-transforming saints who can sing triumphantly, "Bother us, we can cope . . . . through Christ."

> O God, help me to see that men come and go, power structures rise and fall, empires stream across the sky like meteors and sputter out. You alone remain all powerful. Use me today, and always, to cooperate with you until the kingdoms of this world become the kingdoms of our Lord. Amen.

NOTES

1. John Gardner, *Self-Renewal: The Individual and the Innovative Society* (New York: Harper & Row, 1963), p. 5.
2. H. H. Farmer, *The World and God* (New York: Harper & Bros., 1935), p. 196.
3. Oswald Chambers, *My Utmost for His Highest* (New York: Dodd, Mead & Co., 1935), p. 271.
4. Arthur John Gossip, "Revival of Some Obsolete Notes," in *From the Edge of the Crowd*, Arthur John Gossip (Edinburgh: T. & T. Clarke, 1927), p. 33.
5. William Irwin Thompson, *At the Edge of History: Speculations on the Transformation of Culture* (New York: Harper & Row, 1972), p. 230.
6. Harry Emerson Fosdick, *The Meaning of Prayer* (New York: Association Press, 1943), p. 162.
7. Dietrich Bonhoeffer, *Life Together* (New York: Harper & Bros., 1954), p. 99.
8. Malcolm Muggeridge, *Jesus Rediscovered*, (Garden City, N. Y.: Doubleday, 1969), p. 30.
9. Blaise Pascal, *Pensées*.
10. Eric Wollencott Barnes, *The Man Who Lived Twice* (New York: Charles Scribner's Sons, 1956), as quoted in Don Sutherland Bonnell, *Ne Escape from Life* (New York: Harper & Bros., 1958), p. 31.
11. William Hulme, *I Hate to Bother You, But . . .* (St. Louis: Concordia Publishing House, 1970) as quoted in *Take Off Your Shoes* by Mark Link, S.J. (Chicago: Argus Communication, 1972), p. 77.